NO WORDS FOR LOVE AND FAMINE

NO WORDS FOR LOVE AND FAMINE

a novel by
Roberta Morris

CORMORANT BOOKS

Copyright © Roberta Morris, 1993

Published with the assistance of the Canada Council, the Ontario Arts Council, and the support of the Government of Ontario through the Ministry of Culture and Communications.

The author wishes to thank the Ontario Arts Council for its financial support, and Paul Savoie for his help with the French translations and for his abiding friendship.

Edited by Gena K. Gorrell.

Cover image from an oil on canvas, *Untitled — Portrait after Rembrandt*, by Cathy Senitt, from the collection of the Canada Council Art Bank, courtesy of the artist.

Author photo by Julian Kaiser.

Cover design by Artcetera Graphics, Dunvegan, Ontario.

Canadian Cataloguing in Publication Data

Morris, Roberta, 1953-
    No words for love and famine

ISBN 0-920953-53-0

    I. Title.

PS8576.07356N6 1993   C813'.54   C93 - 090330 - 7
PR9199.3.M67N6 1993

Published by
    Cormorant Books Inc.
    RR 1
    Dunvegan, Ontario
    Canada K0C 1J0

For Paul and Ayanna

FOREWORD

Odd, how one inevitably moves backward when writing a foreword, how one gathers, arranges historical material, background, ground back there.

I'm not being a crank; this form does not follow its function. In fact, it contradicts content, and the idea that words name things collapses under the weight of such contradictions.

Still, we can be still. For instance, I could simply shut up.

No, Lois. Forward! The oral form. Get on with it.

Okay. The material in this book was produced from the beginning of 1990 through the spring of '91, but the relationships date back to the beginning of the previous decade. I was a journalist, taking an extended maternity leave after the birth of my second child, ostensibly to expand a collection of articles into a book. Jean-Philippe was working on various translation projects for our mutual publisher, Frances. It was she who arranged for us to meet, explaining to me that J.P. was a fascinating artist, obsessed with language. She told him I had an insatiable curiosity with an intriguing bent for inventive narrative structures, and that there was considerable overlap in his and my interests. From this I surmised that Frances' intention in introducing us was that we might become so absorbed in boring each other we'd stop boring her.

We were all to meet at a benefit poetry reading. I can't recall the cause. Drinks were being served, it was getting late, J.P. was the tenth poet to read, so no one was listening save myself, who felt obliged to remember some key words or phrases for when we met, to flatter him:

> "We agreed not to entertain regrets and I purred praise for your fingertips touching my softest skin and I did not regret my lips forming a moist o in the folds of your skin."

I fell asleep and dreamt that we wrote a book together, half his, half mine, half French, half English, half men's words, half women's, half what we said and half what we did. We began with the ancient knowledge of the poets: whatever we can imagine is possible.

But awake, we began encountering our differences as something other than gifts. J.P.'s project is essentially that of a translator, bringing experience to expression from one language into another, from French into English or, through poetry, from a private to a public language. He grapples with another body, another's body of language, his mother's tongue, whereas I attempt some kind of transliteration, to align sensation with expression, my own body's language with a body of language, a mother's tongue. He thought he could only get translations partially right, but that I would fail entirely in my project, since mine is a misconception of language. J.P. believed that I was attempting to undermine language with language as my only tool, that I would suffer the fate of Archimedes with his fulcrum, inevitable to fail, so at worst (or best) I would simply succeed at destroying my capacity to think.

We both endured slippage, the way language cracks like cement, forming sharp edges that we trip upon and through which grass grows, widening the crack.

Anyway, we did not bore each other. That is not what occurred. We became friends.

Over the next several years Jean-Philippe became increasingly unsettled. Toronto became the focus of his disquiet and he pressed his wife, Margaret, to move with him to Montreal where the cost of living was lower, so he could afford to do less translation work and do more poetry while he lived and worked in his mother tongue. Margaret finally agreed. She quit her job and they moved to Montreal's East Side in December 1989.

By that time I was writing the text for a photo journalist's collected work, including a section on the famine in Ethiopia and Eritrea. Coincidentally, both Jean-Philippe and I had virtually stopped eating:

"Later I chose you for dessert, wanting you the way I sometimes crave live oysters, something slippery that hints of anything but death on the lips."

I'll tell you at the outset, in the time that elapsed during the Sentences and Parole, Jean-Philippe became smaller and then larger, Margaret got bigger and then resumed her normal size, Michael disappeared altogether, I got smaller and to this day am smaller, and the children all got bigger which brings us to a major theme in the correspondence.

PART I. SENTENCES

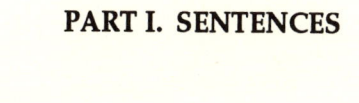

February 5

Dear Jean-Philippe,

Something has happened. I don't know what but something has happened or is happening or is about to happen. I can't shake the sense of it, although everything has taken on a strange stasis around me as if nothing is happening. I haven't been able to either work or eat in days, really not since Michael left for England with the children, and I'm frantic, but

it's not quite correct to say I haven't worked; that depends upon what one considers work. I dusted the furniture, the legs of the furniture, swept cobwebs out of the corners, from between the arms of the chandelier and between the risers and treads on the stairs, vacuumed the carpets. I washed the floors and cleaned the kitchen cupboards. I wiped the refrigerator with Javex, scraped dried lettuce out of vegetable bins, dumped the rusty-looking onions into the garbage. Then I defrosted the freezer section, let the ice melt onto the kitchen floor and washed the floor with the puddled water. The children's clothes are folded, the closets tidied. I cleaned the basement, sorted children's toys and craft materials. Their paraphernalia is now stored neatly in stacked boxes and Michael's tools and scraps of pipe and wood are tidily arranged. The house is immaculate if this counts as work, but

this work is meant to be undone nearly as quickly as it is done. Whole lives are lived between the poles of done and undone housework, yet no one is here except me to mess up the house and I myself am doing nothing to mess it up. The stasis becomes static, a still-life photograph imaging life where life is not happening, and

Michael and the children will be away for three more months. He is taking his training course. The children are visiting with their grandparents. Diane and Daniel will attend an ugly little private school in that ugly little town that they all love so dearly and that I hate so treacherously. We agreed that, all things considered, this would be best, but,

Jean-Philippe, how is it that I am married to an English sales representative who would agree (when we haven't agreed on anything in years) that, to avoid a terrible row (to which I would not succumb in any event; I am not a coward but would rather withstand silence), the children ought to get to know their grandparents better and I ought to have time to work in a concentrated manner, so he, Michael, ought to take the children with him to England when he takes his course? This is what we finally agreed upon so I can finish William's book, so I will have time to think. But how can one think when so much time spills out over a whole day? I'm sitting here with William's photos spread out on the kitchen table, knowing that it isn't raining in Eritrea, that people are planting despite the war, but I have no connection except these photos, images of what has happened but is no longer happening, not like that, because it has been happening ever since. I have no way of really knowing what is happening. God damn, Jean, what is happening? Answer me that?

Calm down,

that's what you'd say. I know. I wish we could talk. I miss meeting you for coffee at Tasty's, the two of us eavesdropping on drunken conversations just as the drunks eavesdropped on ours. I even miss those awkward occasions when you and Margaret brought dessert over in the evening and the four of us watched a video and drank wine once the children were settled into bed. How Margaret and Michael loathed those evenings, didn't they? And how I loathed Margaret's baking, and you Michael's company. You and I do better on our own. Between the four of us there were six relationships, one of which was happy, and

how peculiar our happiness must appear to people who spend

their lives, as Margaret and Michael did, in offices where one settles in at nine in the morning, tea taken at ten-thirty while one stands by the pot passing one's time in comfortable chatter until one returns to one's desk until lunch when one leaves for an hour with or without a co-worker, after which one sits down for another few hours of work or whatever one does at one's desk until the afternoon coffee break, a timely interruption before one finishes off the day and then goes home to a spouse who enquires each and every day, "How was your day, dear?" It is so easy and must be incomprehensible to them, why you and I meeting for coffee together could be such a happy event,

before you left. Now I must stay calm. I have to think. I'm fine. It's February and like the bulbs in my garden I should be soaking up nutrients so I will be ready for spring. This happens every year.

To relieve myself of myself last night I went to Bloor Cinema and saw *Rebel Without a Cause*. I saw it years ago when I was absorbed in Freudian psychology and what struck me then was the crude presentation of the Freudian model, which typified the period and dated the film. But watching it again and having recently read so much about the sexual abuse of children, what now struck me was that, in the first twenty minutes of the film, Natalie Wood's character (whose name I can't remember because to me Natalie Wood is forever an icon of Natalie Wood) and the girl's father exhibited six or seven signs of incest, and that was all I could see. When I considered this, that what matters to me is all that I can see, I became afraid. If this is true, won't I sink into my own obsessions inevitably? How can it be otherwise, and why am I not already mad?

What movies have you seen lately? I can't imagine. Montreal seems far away. I know I can go down to the Island Airport and be there in forty-five minutes, but I know I won't go down to the Island and won't be in Montreal, that this distance is not measured in kilometres that can simply be eaten up by time in an aircraft. It is a distance of dailiness, compounded by the syntax of our two languages, such that now, even if you tell me what movies you see or what books you read, your ideas about the books and movies are transmuted into another grammar; I will not really know what you think; I will know a little *about* it but not *it*. And I have no one to blame but myself for my ignorance of your mother tongue. I should have paid more attention to my high school French teachers

but I never paid one bit of attention, not to a single teacher, not a bit of attention. I regret that now. If I'd ever paid any serious attention to anyone out there maybe I would understand what is happening and I could wrest a book out of that understanding but

what difference does it make if I don't understand what is happening now since nothing is happening? Jean-Philippe, tell me what you think.

Love, Lois

*

                                                             10 February
Dear Lois,

    What do I think? I think perhaps I should write to Michael and explain that he must return home immediately so that you can fight with him about your writing instead of fighting yourself. I'm sure I could present your predicament in such cogent terms even Michael wouldn't fail to understand, but you must provide me with his address. When was it decided that he would go to England with the children? I didn't even hear the possibility mentioned before your last letter.

You want to know what is happening here. We found this apartment near Duluth and St-Denis and we took it. It's all openings and doorways but there's no doors. The ancient carport beneath the bedroom is not insulated so cold air blows up between the floorboards. I've taken to sleeping on the sofa in the living room. Margaret prefers to sleep in our bed beneath a pile of blankets and remains there most of the days, reading trash fiction. When I suggest she might go out and explore the city she replies that she's seen snow. There are interesting spots in Montreal, I tell her, galleries, the botanical garden, shopping. She looks at me as if I'm insane. Leave me alone, she tells me, I'm reading. I suggest she might sit in the living room to read by natural light. She suggests I go to the library to write. I can't bear to see you like this, I bray. Then go to the library, she repeats. Usually I go out later, late enough so that we are both sure that my leaving has little to do with her suggestion, that I'm not being booted out.

Why the hell did we take this place? I should have been more sensitive to my wife's needs. We saw a lovely apartment above Sherbrooke near McGill. Margaret might have been happy on the other side of the city, and I could have spent all my time wandering away from there. I remember saying that this neighbourhood seemed more real, whatever the hell that means, other than that Margaret would be miserable here.

You needn't worry about the language barrier between us—you are such a romantic, Lois—because we are focused on the same issue, food. Our publisher suggested you write a text for famine photos while I'm starving, living with a woman of insatiable appetite. I think Margaret has put on ten pounds since we moved here, and I have lost the same amount of weight because it makes me sick to watch her eat. We are situated near a number of decent restaurants but Margaret prefers to walk down towards the Main for take-out, Harvey's hamburgers, fries and shakes until I think I am going to vomit. Yesterday she brought home fishburgers and fries which I did eat and I did vomit.

I suggest we go out to a movie but she won't come so I go alone. Last week I went to the Rialto and, like you, saw *Rebel Without a Cause* but I did not see incest. I saw the play of homoeroticism between Jimmy and Plato, knowing as we all now know James Dean's sexual orientation. Odd, we went to the same film but saw it, of course, differently. Yet, coincidence is the glue in our friendship, the two of us sitting in the dark three hundred miles apart, watching a film we intend to discuss with each other later.

But you returned home alone and I returned home to Margaret. She acted betrayed that I'd leave her alone at night when she has no friends here and can't even phone for a pizza because she is terrified to speak French and horrified that she can't anyway. There was a box of pizza lying open and half-eaten on the counter so I shouted, "But you did order pizza." "Yes, I ordered a pizza and they sent it to me. So if this is a victory, why are you screaming at me?"

I am confounded. The fact is, I don't miss you; I don't miss Toronto; I don't miss anything but my sleep and peace of mind because Margaret is driving me crazy with her carrying on about how she hates it here until I just want to be left alone but if I leave her alone she acts as if I've committed some terrible crime. How can I leave her alone with nothing to do and no place to go, she bellows, and of course she never leaves me alone here because she never leaves at all, except for her Harvey's run. In this apartment we live like two rats in a maze; we can find neither each other nor the exit.

God, I am hungry. I should eat something. I'll go out and get myself a beer and some food, and then get down to work on that translation, starting tonight. That's what's happening,

avec amitié, J.P.

*

February 16

Jean-Philippe,

and do you want me to write to Margaret and tell her to stop eating before you starve yourself to death? No? No, and don't write Michael

and no, I don't find it amusing that you are starving yourself while Margaret eats herself sick while I'm writing about people starving. This is not even interesting. This is stupid. It is the pornography of plenty that you would compare your and Margaret's eating problems with those of people who have no food. I would write (if I could write at all) about real hunger, which is altogether different from your neurotic relationship to Margaret and to food. There are no metaphors for famine, or love, birth or death;

some things are basic. I can barely approach these words and so I try to say "that is like this", because I can't stand up to the fact that this is only this and cannot be that; this just is.

Yes. Love is like famine that way. Remember that night on the phone? you on the other end of the line when all we had was speech, and I told you another man had said I was like a man and the electrons carrying what was almost the same as your words told me not to be offended; it's only a metaphor. I raised a feeble protest, looking down at my breasts under my loose night-shirt, noticing the small wrinkles near my nipples left by men and babies who sucked until the glands expanded and then shrank back. I wanted to lift my skirt up and show you. I was sitting cross-legged without underpants, so I might have looked like a fruit bowl, but I am not a fruit bowl; I am a woman and this is not a metaphor for anything. The problem was that we were talking on the phone and there was only speech.

(Mary Ellmann points out quite correctly I think, in her book *Thinking About Women*, that there is nothing like hunger but hunger. "What could I say about men and women in India? Food has all the authority in starvation," she says and because she is writing about sexual politics she puts that in perspective. "Sexual politics and sexual opinions, and I suppose sexuality itself, are all fringe benefits of eating.") There is hunger and there is hunger, I suppose, but there is only hunger if it is yours and you are really starving, and

I can't write about that; I can't even get my mind around such words. It is only one section of William's collection and besides, this is non-fiction I'm writing; it's a simple matter of making choices between supposed facts and the words should be easy. Common sense dictates; words name things or actions or sensations like hunger. I know these words and I also know they can make me some money. They are referents, just as a photo refers directly to the image it depicts. It should be easy to refer more or less directly to the direct referents to which the images refer and, using glue words to hold the referents together, to make sentences that appear to represent but actually construct the world, or at least aspects of the world, what I affectionately call *out there*. (I believe this about photos, that they are direct references, but not words, which might be the reason I often find the text of picture books muddled. The words contradict the image. The image proves *this is* while the words beg the question *are you sure?*)

Yes, words fail me. You remember my friends' baby, Gregory? I was watching him, almost one year old, learn his first word, "dog", abbreviated "da". We were at High Park, his family and mine, and Gregory pointed to a dog and tried to form his mouth to say "da" while our other four children ran around him, challenging him, "Say 'dog' Gregory. Say 'dog'." And their attention, like Gregory's, shifted away from the dog, away from the word, toward the sound of the word, so in time the dog itself seemed hardly to matter at all; the sound was everything.

What is the magic that transcends the banality of words naming things, like Eritrea and famine, that promises to connect us to everything including God if we trace the sound, one word meaning many things, perhaps everything, if we can only follow the sound long enough, far enough? Enough. It eludes us. It promises more,

a visceral response. Some words I hear first near my stomach, like a hunger but not hunger, so when my son says, "Mom, I'm hungry. Fix me some eggs for breakfast, please," my body responds and I have a job to do, to appease my son's hunger, and an infinite amount of food for thought. My attention shifts away from the task of making breakfast, to the odd hissing of the dragged out *please* that has no essential naming power but some other power that corresponds to the hunger next to my stomach, which compelled me almost every morning to fry my son an egg with all that an egg means, call it love

and then empty that word of meaning, because that word is the same one Michael uses to name a particular attachment, his penis reaching down into my body, a word with a web of meanings that trap us just as I am trapped beneath the meaning of his body, and it is the word I use with my son and I do not want him the way Michael wants me, and it is the same word I use when I pray but then I say it like a mantra until I can think without words into an infinite stillness that excludes my son whom I say I love and my work which I love but cannot do and Michael who uses the word to mean he wants me

(I know what you're thinking: *it really means you should join him in England*)

which is a long way of getting to my point: I'm having a hell of a time writing this text. There's the photographs, historical information, geographical and climatic conditions recorded, but the largest section, the photos taken in Eritrea, confound me. There's a woman in one photograph and her and my world is mediated by impossible words (and by that impossible man, William, and by his camera) so I don't even know how to begin. Poor Gregory, he can learn the words but it won't help.

Love, Lois

*

20 February

Dear Lois,

Last night I found myself in Foufounes, a small pitcher of beer in my right hand, quarters for a pool game in my left, watching some girls attempting a lesbian experiment at the pool table. I had no wish to interfere, except in their game. I placed my quarters on the edge of their table and sat back to watch. They stared at me. These days, at best I look professional, my clothes hanging loosely from my diminished frame, but last night I did not look my best. I looked lost among the students in black leather and green hair, one who drifted up from the street sniffing out their youth, hungry. I was hungry, and descended to the street, leaving the girls my quarters for their next game. I needed real food. On the corner of St-Laurent and Ste-Catherine within one block there's a Dunkin' Donuts, Harvey's, McDonald's and a Burger King, video palaces and strip bars—surely Margaret and I can find happiness together here—*jouissance*, his and hers. This thought depressed me. I went home and fell asleep on the sofa.

Margaret put on more weight, I know, but she says it is none of my damn business. It is my business. I can't sleep with a woman who has achieved such dimension. She is very large, but appears suddenly small again when she crawls beneath her duvets with her romance novels and detective stories stacked around her bed as if they were bricks around a castle's moat, she so small she almost disappears. There is a mythical creature I dimly recall who changes size like this. Margaret is becoming a fast-food–eating, fire-breathing dragon, and it wouldn't matter if we spoke English or French to each other now because we don't speak to each other at all. I finally understand her consumption. It is an act of aggression. She hates me for bringing her to Montreal, to a city where she doesn't speak the language and is without work or friendship, for taking this apartment with no doors. She will do me in, beginning with sex, but eventually by taking up all the space in the apartment until I no longer exist here at all.

This being said, I do not intend to whine to you any longer on the subject of Margaret's and my problem. It is clearly annoying you, although I must say, your problems are not so different or more interesting.

Poor Gregory? Poor Michael, who says he loves you, and poor Frances who wants a book outline from you and not all your thoughts about why you can't write it. You're a rare bird, a commercially viable writer, which is why she gave you the assignment. You said it yourself: this should be easy. The contradiction you note between words and images is not impenetrable; the logic of literacy extends to photography, perhaps has achieved some sort of perfection, in fact, with the invention of the camera, whose subject is pure projection, chemically appropriated so the photographer can hold it, famine if you will, in his left hand and a Big Mac in his right.

Ah, but maybe famine isn't an appropriate subject for those born lucky. Disasters, war and drought are occasions of cataclysm in which you drown or rise. Not us; we rise because it's morning and easy or we fail to rise. It hardly matters, but the choice is ours, to take form strong as concrete or dissolve. Yet concrete is weird, poured and made hard by water while water has no essential form. Irony is inherent in life for those born lucky, like us.

We are so much alike but we decide on opposing resolutions concerning form. I confound matter with multiplication, one times an infinity of possibilities. You confound it with division, breaking it up until there are no words to describe it, until it is reduced to a wail. The choice is ours. There is no war or famine, no form but the matter shaped by decision for those born lucky.

No, Lois, I can't concede that it eludes metaphor; the resolution is the same; we drown or rise.

However, I do not suggest you join Michael in England. I presume nothing, recognizing that we are now both living outside our desire. At least we have our work and, as you say, this should be easy. You also say that the more you think about your subject the more stupid you feel. I'm afraid it is the case that the more you think about it the more stupid you become, my friend.

Si tu savais.... Tu penses donc tu n'es pas. Tu fais peut-être ton entrée dans une pièce et cherches où t'asseoir. Tu fais quelques pas et tu t'accroches le genou contre une chaise mais tu te rends quand même jusqu'à la fenêtre. Tu te penches contre le chambranle, te perches tant bien que mal sur le rebord. J'aimerais bien que tu trouves la position qui te convienne le mieux mais j'ai le vertige rien qu'à penser au mal que tu te feras en tombant du sixième étage et en allant te fracasser le crâne contre le béton.

Je t'embrasse, J.P.

*

February 27

Dear Jean-Philippe,

one month has passed of the three months that Michael and the children will be away, which now will actually be five months because Michael thinks the children should finish their school term in England, since their studies are going quite well. Okay, I can be reasonable. The children, as if to console me, say they miss me and want to come home although they know I need this time to work, blah blah blah... while Michael assumes I am having a holiday, thinking of the children as he does, as so much work

which is not the way I think of them at all; they have never been a job for me. Even when Diane and Daniel were babies and would cry at night, I could roll over to bring them towards my breast and I didn't mind; this was not work. They'd suck and fall off to sleep and only later was it framed as a problem, and then not by me but by Michael, who was amazed that I could sleep with a child sucking on my breast. He said that if anyone woke him up so often (even if it was little baby Jesus) he'd be enraged. He was grateful that he didn't have to go about getting bottles warmed in the middle of the night, but shouldn't babies be put on a feeding schedule? I resisted. I was a tree in a certain season, my children were fruit (we have words for this: the apple of my eye) and it was easy. Perhaps you, like Michael, find it impossible to believe. Almost everyone does. Mother has become a job and a bad job at that, something you might choose but probably wouldn't, hence the emphasis on control, birth control. I didn't choose to become a mother or choose not to become a mother. It was an act of appalling passivity by modern standards. A chorus of modern voices urged me to take control of my own body, could not accept my choice to relinquish control, to simply be my body, which twice has also meant to be with child as well, but

why am I defending myself to you? You are utterly beside the point (on purpose) which brings me to the point I wanted to make at the outset:

it is fitting that you scrawl your pejorative judgements in a language I barely comprehend, since your idea of me has everything to do with you and nothing to do with me (hence nothing to do with the vocabulary we share) so it's fine. Express yourself to yourself in what functions between us as your private language. I will not labour to translate or respond. I have my own private language. Last night I dreamt it, drew out my perceptions of your folly in a kind of Arabic script with the curls of my hair and my nail clippings. You would understand neither the content nor the form, no more than I understand French, and this was fine; the dream really had nothing to do with you. It was private, and

when I woke up I was able to transpose the energy of the dream onto the written page as intelligent prose (an alchemy I've mastered) (thank you). I spread out William's photos and scratched out a series of subtexts on pieces of paper that I clipped to each photo. My notes are unrelated to William's journalistic reporting. It's not that I disbelieve him, his account of the liberation struggle, the character of Haile Selassie and now Mengistu, the geo-political issues related to famine, but this simply has nothing to do with the pictures. The photos consist of a chemical effect. Grammatically speaking, they (as subject) are (meaning that *they* exist) William's (possessive) photos (the complement). Put another way (I will try again with you), Roland Barthes's point: words aren't direct referents; language is by nature fictional, mediated. My notes construct reality other than William's. I pick and choose among his unconscious metaphors ("When I shot that photo, I knew I'd never buy white bread again," etc.), which is all I can get from him. What I wanted was unrelated to his intent of *seeing* things for me; I wanted to know if the metal on the gun was hot since the air was hot (metal always feels cold to me, at least in memory); I wanted recipes and to know what these people would have been doing if there hadn't been a famine and a war. Then I would know what they are hungry for and what they are fighting for. That's how I'd organized my outline which Frances didn't accept in any case, it being nothing like what she had in mind for the outset. Fine. Today

it's Diane's birthday. I sent a cake and a blue angora sweater which I thought might remind her of the Canadian sky on a clear day; they don't have such days in England, at least not in that dreary little town. I'm sorry if I sound testy.

Love, Lois

*

6 March

Dear Lois,

My apologies for having offended you with my previous letter, and thank you for your letter. You put a pleasant face on motherhood and, knowing that if anything can arouse desire in a woman for a man it is another woman waxing prosaic about the wonders of child-bearing, I showed your letter to Margaret. She broke down and cried. I was amazed. Lately she's displayed no emotion except angry temper or indifference, if indifference can be called an emotion, not simply the lack thereof. I was touched, literally and figuratively. I couldn't believe my luck. You'd brought me luck. Everything was going to be fine, I thought, but then noticed something strange. My recalcitrant member didn't twitch with excitement although the rest of my body was twitching with insatiable need; it had been so long. I need it, yes, but need is not the same as desire. Desire is dead here, Lois.

Once that fact was mutually recognized, and given the circumstances it could hardly be disguised, Margaret and I had The Talk. She explained in halting language, as if she were hauling each word up like a log from a mucky river bottom, that she was not in fact overweight and that our problem was simply in my imagination. "I am five feet four inches and weigh approximately 135 pounds, that is 61 kilos, and that is fine according to the weight charts, my doctor and myself. If you have a problem with me, it is in your imagination. It is your problem, in fact, not mine. Nevertheless, we do have a problem."

I protested. "You are actually bigger, Margaret. That is a simple fact, not a metaphor."

"My dear," she said," can't anything be what it is and like something else." This statement filled me with utter confusion. Is everyone a philosopher this year?

Lois, I swear Margaret has put on several pounds and this is why I do not find her sexually attractive. Now, why would she lie about something like that? I continued quarrelling with her, "You seem larger than life to me," to which she replied that perhaps she needed more muscle tone. She would start doing sit-ups if I would make love with her again. Then I reminded her that she might not take this so personally, that I have been preoccupied with my work since our move to Montreal, to which she replied, "What work?"

Now Margaret has signed up to take a French class at McGill, beginning in April. She joined a health club and is seeing her doctor about a proper diet. She will also look for a job, although our present economic circumstances don't necessitate more income and with her limited French finding work will be difficult. Regardless, since she sleeps until noon and will soon be occupied most afternoons with her classes I'll have time alone to work. So once again, thank you for writing. You helped us achieve some resolution.

Love, J.P.

*

22 March

Dear Lois,

When I didn't receive a response to my last letter I became concerned and tried to contact you on the phone over several days with no luck. Perhaps I'm alarmist, but the voice that comes through your writing lately is vague and has become increasingly vague. Pardon me, but complexity and vacuity are almost interchange\able for this reader. It is my own limitation; I don't want to impose upon you my taste for the tightly constructed paragraph, but now you don't even answer your phone. I am concerned. Call me collect, or respond to this letter at your earliest convenience so that I will relax.

Love, J.P.

*

April 1

Dear Jean-Philippe,

as Frances indicated when you phoned her (that was quite unnecessary, J.P.) my work is progressing and there is no cause for concern. I was sufficiently lucid to satisfy her, if not you. I spent five weeks alone;

that is all. I left the phone unplugged except late at night when Michael or the children might try to call, and since my answering machine was being serviced no one could reach me. I am sorry if I am an unsatisfactory correspondent but I have spent this time thinking about the project, producing notes and revised outline that I gave to Frances. Now I am ready to write.

I will begin soon.

During the week in which your alarm seems to have reached a fevered pitch I'd spent a few days visiting the Eritrean Relief Association's office here in Toronto and found several photo essays that stand in stark contrast to William's work. The revolutionaries produce, almost exclusively, images of happy people, hungry or not, intact or without limbs. I'm tempted to think of them as the photographic reincarnation of Socialist Realist paintings, but in Eritrea the socialist Soviets fight against the socialist liberation army, and can everyone be happy? The contrast between their images and William's completely confounds me. What is real exists outside the frame of the lens,

somewhere out there which I know nothing about. Yesterday a friend dropped by, a mere acquaintance of Michael's whom I barely recognized, a client whom Michael has known since high school, someone who apparently was concerned much the way you were when I could not be reached by phone, although I still don't know why he tried. I served him tea and he told me a great deal about his business, clothing manufacturing, something I know nothing about. Last night I dreamt I was writing a book about people who have no clothes.

Today the day is wet and the window is not clear. Still I can see when I look and I keep looking even though I have work to do and need to concentrate. I can't. There's part of my thoughts that go outside the window and part of my thoughts that are directed towards my computer screen,

my work. My work is easy now, today, but I can't do it. It is under my control but my thoughts are not; they wander to where I am not (out there). Out there is what I know nothing about, except what I see through the window which is mostly just wet leaves and spots because the window needs wiping. There are many things I know nothing about out there (this I know), but today I think about only one thing out there because it has been such a long winter. I could think about Orota or sorghum or economic development (which I know nothing about) but I don't I think about my visitor out there. He came in here

like an apparition with whom I was familiar. I could welcome him without fear since now he was in here. We could talk and laugh and in here it seemed as if we knew what we were talking about. Then we shook hands and it seemed as if we knew who we were touching. It was easy in here. Then he went out there,

which is confusing for me. In here there were two of us, one about whom I really know nothing but it seemed I did because he was in here, just as when you or Michael or the children were in here. If there is someone in here with me, for instance when my visitor was here, there is a chance I can understand what is going on; out there, there isn't a chance. Now with him out there I can, at best, only half understand. What was in here is now half out there

and makes me a little afraid, not because I am a coward necessarily but because it is half unknown and there is always some fear of the unknown which, for me, is everything out there,

but I am only half afraid. Actually, it's none of my business. What is in here is my business, even love in here, but love or curiosity or disgust or a decision to forget all about what is out there is none of my business if it is out there, unless I choose to make it my business, say, choose to write a book about people who have no clothes,

and I do not choose this. The computer screen glows and I try to concentrate on what is in here, my notes on the discussions with William. As if by some miracle I do concentrate and thoughts constellate into a paragraph. At first it is just a few letters, but then it is a whole word and then a sentence and eventually it is a whole paragraph,

a good one. I look back towards the window. The window is a frame, framing out there. But the frame frames only what I can see out there. My visitor, for instance, is out there but out there is not framed for him as it is framed for me. It has a different frame or perhaps no frame if he is taking a stroll in the great outdoors. Perhaps out there is delineated for him by the horizon

which is something I know nothing about, nor can I know so long as I stay in here

and I am fine in here, so stop worrying about me.

Love, Lois

*

7 April

Dearest Lois,

Thanks for finally answering my letter, although Frances did her best to convince me that you were, as always, fine. My work continues to go smoothly. I suppose Frances told you she found another project for me, a bilingual anthology of Canadian poetry. It might make her company a pretty penny if it's ordered in bulk by the Montreal and Toronto school boards. That's her target. The translation is demanding as it will be examined by every reader, the French on the left, English on the right, but literary translation is not without its rewards. I'm still bored yet it is not the work that bores me; I bore myself.

I spend days now walking through Montreal, a translator's dream, English and French spoken on the street so that the two tones sometimes produce one note, simultaneously an opposition and a synthesis. It astonishes me, my sisters' willingness to relinquish this birthright and forget their mother tongue. I asked Mireille once, "Doesn't it bother you that you can hardly speak to your own mother now?" and she laughed, "No. It's a fucking relief."

I hesitate to recommend any reading to you now that you've finally begun to sit down and write, although it sounds as if your visitor has already distracted you, diverting your concentration on foreigners' gastronomic hunger to your own hunger of another sort. Anyway, if you are not already familiar with it, Sontag's essay *On Photography* might interest you. She argues that the entire enterprise of the concerned photographer is defeated by the medium itself; photography can't motivate political change; it simply documents it. If you agree, it follows that William's intentions are beside the point; your work is to complement the documentation. Adopt your old journalist's style and borrow a good history book. That is my advice, which you specifically did not request.

Today I played a small trick on Margaret to get her out of the house, since I had some work to finish. She woke us at noon, as usual. I can't imagine how she sleeps so soundly at night, having done little with the day, when I can hardly sleep after a full morning's work at my desk, an afternoon's work at the library, then spending the evening until the early hours of the morning out walking. She sleeps soundly, eating and reading herself into restful oblivion, one romance novel after another pizza. I asked her about this newly acquired taste for genre fiction and she readily agreed that it is repetitious, claiming that this is indeed its appeal; the repetition of an essentially pleasurable experience, like eating or sex, is its pleasure. Anyway, the trick: I asked if she'd go pick up Marie-Claire Blais's *Les voyageurs sacrés* at L'Androgyne, thinking it amusing if Margaret walked into a French gay and lesbian book store to pick up an uncut book, another phenomenon I assumed she had never encountered. I scratched the title of the book and the address of the book store on a scrap of paper and said no more about it, chuckling to myself as she went out the door. Two hours later she returned, handed me the volume and told me she'd had a delightful conversation with the store's owner, who recommended Jean Cocteau's *White Book*, which she also purchased. She read Cocteau's book immediately and is now making her way through Blais's, armed with a knife in one hand, her French/English dictionary in the other, safe from the spring chill with her duvets piled around her on our bed. I have to get out of here to get some work done. Keep in touch.

    Love, J.P.

*

13 April
Dear Lois,

    Perhaps you're not writing letters because you're writing your text. Frances gave it to you as a bread-and-butter job, and treated as such it could be finished in a month, and then perhaps you'll answer my letters.

    Margaret discovered Schwartz's, an infamous deli around the corner. I recognized the smell on her clothing immediately and then on her breath. "You've been to Schwartz's," I accused. "Yes, and I brought you a pickle," she twinkled, extracting from her pocket an embalmed cucumber wrapped in beige paper. Her mood is shifting, lifting, and suddenly she's crazy for sex. Simultaneously, as if we had to maintain a malevolent equilibrium, a mean spirit is overtaking me. I walk in front of it, keeping just one step ahead. I walk a very long time, a long distance. The libraries are mere waystations; I try to maintain a balance between the exhaustion in my head and in my legs. I walk from one library to another, to find my way by late afternoon into a bar, to sit with a beer by a window so I can watch other people walking. I walk until my intestines swell with gas, until walking becomes a self-imposed torture. At night if I walk north towards the Plateau I can find a bar with some respectable music, hoping that if I listen I will become respectable, that there is an acoustical equivalent of the maxim "You are what you eat." But more often I walk south and along Ste-Catherine, dropping into Foufounes with its flying skeletons that bespeak Art at its most youthful, or into Casanova's for a steamie. Usually I can't eat so I drink coffee to keep awake. I can sit there and watch the scene, the queen eating her poutine, by the door the leggings that smile as I leave. I am not lost nor has anything gone missing. I know my loneliness will still be there when I get back to it, be right where I left it, but I don't want to go home yet.

And how is everything with you?

Love, J.P.

*

20 April

Dear Lois,

Still you don't reply. I wish I kept a copy of my last letter. I think I might have offended you. Please do not be offended, and I won't bore you further with my problems. I think about you often, while you apparently think about me seldom if at all, if one can judge by the scarcity of mail. Do I rave? I will not rave today. I am calm.

Basically, as a favour to you and Frances, I met William last week for lunch. He was in from Vancouver, on his way back to Africa I think he said, but actually I can't recall. I asked Margaret if she cared to join us, but she refused. To tell the truth, that pleased me, to invite her and to have her refuse, because she embarrasses me. She looks dowdy even if she is, in fact, a creature of immense love and hate. The switch she affects between appearances and actuality intimidates strangers. It was a dragon like her, not an empathetic demigod Prometheus, but a dragon who blew on us and gave us fire. I am sure this is true; I saw it in a dream.

Anyway, Frances was convinced that when William's west coast warmth met Montreal's chilly manner it would result in fog, so she asked me to put a happy face on our intellectual community and show William around Montreal a bit. He and I agreed, in a phone conversation, to meet at Mme Hoang's Épicerie. I go there often on my way to the Central Library. I enjoy the dimensions of the building and the large tiffany window above the door. I sat down at the table facing the window, my usual, a two-foot marble square on a wrought-iron pedestal, to wait for William to blow in. I recognized him immediately from your descriptions. After cursory introductions he announced that he was feeling peckish and ordered two of the day's special, although I told him I would just have soup and coffee. The table was soon piled up with books, our hats and gloves, his greatcoat, my jacket, and then two bowls of soup, the salads, brochettes de crevettes, tarts and finally two coffees. He started helping the waitress arrange everything, his booming voice bouncing off the tile floors and plate glass windows. A room of duvets wouldn't stifle this voice and Mme Hoang hadn't so much as a cloth serviette to do the job. The waitress seemed amused. Not I. He talked incessantly while I sipped, first my soup and then my coffee, and before I might have conveyed one bit of information about Montreal, he was piling back into his coat, offering to pay for the meal. I threw down five dollars, and followed him out the door. If he didn't learn anything while he was here I don't think he noticed. He sends you his regards.

I picked up Roland Barthes's *Camera Lucida; Reflections on Photography*, basically so that I'd have something to discuss with you in this letter. Your friend, Barthes, makes an important point: a photo documents a particular moment so that one might say that what it represents really existed, but then exists as an object, while what it represents no longer exists, at least not as it is represented. Thus the photograph distorts time as it is existentially experienced. Moments aren't supposed to be anything but fleeting. Otherwise they are an hour or an epoch or a photograph of a moment. I see your problem. When you are looking at William's photo of a starving person, you might accept it as documenting that person's hunger, but that person was only hungry like that for an instant. In the next instant the person either obtained food or was more hungry. That particular moment of hunger, if you take the hungry person more seriously than the photograph, is rather inconsequential. It is the experience of hunger, the web of hungriness, I suppose, that is troubling. A photograph serves to reduce knowing, or our notion of what it is to know, to seeing an object, the photograph. Knowing is more; it involves understanding, judgement and, dare we admit it, commitment. Ultimately, I suppose, knowing involves love. But what you have are only photos which at best capture the banality of war and starvation. Seeing them, we can believe that we know something about famine while this so-called knowledge changes nothing.

Unfortunately, William's photographs, at least the few I've seen, are intrinsically interesting. He is a good photographer in the sense that the limitations of his work are not apparent. Personally I applaud the movement in photography away from that style, even away from technical competence. The blurry subject, caught in the moment when the photographer was losing his balance, might be the most essentially photographic.

But am I boring you, Lois? I bore myself so I will stop. Please write soon. I have something more I need to ask you.

Sincerely, J.P.

*

27 April

Dear Lois,

I am almost reduced to begging you to respond. My situation is deteriorating, and it would be good of you to show some interest. I cannot sleep at night, get up two hours before the sun, and with this abundance of time my solitude forms whorls, as if everything exists as surface tension. At best I achieve viscosity. The only solid object is this fucking pen. I hold it as Odysseus held the mast—I am tied to it—and with it I scrawl off a note to you but there is no response.

Margaret has decided that I am having an affair. She vacillates between remorse and fury. Last Saturday we went to the Cathedral together, ostensibly to listen to music but I knew she was after—a confession. The last organ note's echo died into the vaulted ceiling and, while we slipped on our coats, I wondered, regrettably aloud, why someone as passionate as I am about music is left passionless by church music, wanting neither to fuck nor to pray. Now, if I had one bit of sense, knowing what Margaret was after, I would never have raised the subject of fucking, but what is done is done. "How come, Jean," she hissed, "when all you think about is fucking, you don't fuck me? Well, I know why; what I don't know is her name." "Whose name? What are you talking about?" I protested. "Oh, fuck yourself. Shit, Jean, we're in church."

You might think I could have left it at that. People were staring, but I stuck my face right in front of her to make her see me. "Okay, Ms. Reverent, you tell me why God made us with these vacillating passions. So we could tear each other's eyes out?" "I don't think so," she smiled. I suppose she saw people staring. "I think it's so sometimes men and women can be very happy."

Margaret now insists that I need to see a psychiatrist. She blames my condition on a latent Catholicism that condemns me to misery. She might be right but then, don't you think, both Freud's and the Church Fathers' teachings are equally correct. If God is our projection, it is the other side of the same coin, minted in Western theology, that we are God's projection, created in God's image. Does that not suggest to you that God is as tight-fisted and limp-dicked as I am? Then God needs me, the mirror to reflect back to God that God is a pathetic middle-aged man, and what can a psychiatrist say to ameliorate that?

Rather than present this argument to her, I tried to explain to Margaret the complexities of emotion she constellates within me. Her interjections were no help. I explain, "You seem larger than life to me," and she suggests we make love with the lights off. In the end I lie, claiming I am simply preoccupied with my work, this translation. Tonight it was Margaret who went out.

I suppose I should see a doctor. Please write when you have a moment.

Love, J.P.

*

30 April

Dear Lois,

Still no word from you and, when I tried to call, the operator informed me that your phone has been disconnected. I won't contact Frances again, but please write. I won't argue with you. I just want to know what is happening with you.

Yesterday I wandered into a video arcade that smelled of wet leather and cigarettes. I was the oldest man in there, save the man in the token booth. Lately I notice everyone's age. I bought some tokens and sat down at the "Thunder Blade", a game that looks like a snowmobile with a joy stick jutting up between your legs. There's nothing subtle in a video arcade. You shoot when you see the title "Mission Begins". I played for two hours until I was finally hungry.

Last night Margaret and I made love, but then she woke up this morning accusing me of using my prick as a cattle prod that did indeed shock her. God, Lois, there are times when we are rough with each other but we come up bruised and happy. This was different; this time she was not happy and, come to think of it, I was not bruised.

Damn it, Lois, I hope you are doing something effective about Eritrea's famine that makes you so indifferent to the local variety. You could have stopped me from doing something quite destructive, but you chose to ignore me. So be it. I don't care if you answer my letters any more.

I'll stop now. J.P.

*

April 28

Dear Jean-Philippe,

you ask me why I haven't answered any of your letters. Here. I will try now. I haven't written or spoken more than a word at a time for weeks, and only one word, so the effort now is exhausting. I must rest now.

May 3

You ask me why i haven't answered any of your letters. I will try to explain. I hadn't received them. Or more accurately, they were received but not by me and i didn't read them. He gathered up my mail and filed it away for me. He asked, "You don't want to read these just now, do you? Do you want me to put them in the file with the rest of your mail?" and i answered, yes.

May 4

Today i received another letter from you. Thanks. You have been more than patient. I'll try to answer your questions. I'm happy, you might say. Yes, i would say i am happy so this is not depression, this strange wordlessness. "Are you happy?" He asks. Why does He ask? Surely He would know if i wasn't happy. I reply with the only word i have at my disposal, yes. That is all i've been able to say for weeks now, yes. Perhaps He is framing his questions such that yes is the only appropriate reply. Yes, certainly it seems appropriate enough. I suppose

you want to know more about Him. He is my age almost exactly, greying hair and skin more fair than mine. He is about six foot tall. I am pushing out words now to say something about him and it is exhausting. It seems as if i've known him almost all my life so i am surprised you two have never met, but i realize you haven't, so that's that. You don't know him but you know of him,

i think. I mentioned a visitor in my last letter to you. He is smart, yes. He is smart enough to phrase his questions so as to always get an affirmative response. That might be what has happened. When he helped me pack, when he took me to his place and asked if he could kiss me goodnight, of course i said yes. That was a month ago

and i have hardly crawled out of his bed since that night. "You don't need to work today, do you? You can rest some more," He says. "Yes," i say but

in fact i feel so well rested my legs can hardly move. It's as if a virus attacked my muscles but this isn't a virus; my own body has paralysed itself like some strange autoimmunity, immune to the reflexes that tighten and allow movement.

"I'll bring you breakfast. Would you like some eggs and toast?" "Yes."

Is this bliss, i ask myself? Yes. Everything I need is attended to and before i had been so cruelly exhausted; nothing made any sense. The necessity of moving, for instance, made no sense. The landlord had written to Michael to inform us that her family was taking over the house, and this Michael had not told me until the very last minute because he didn't know what to tell me, which makes no sense except that he was trying to decide whether he was coming back and he has decided he is not coming back himself and is not sending the children back, and this my visitor knew before i did which also makes no sense except business sense; they are colleagues. I guess there is a lawsuit pending. I am afraid i will lose so it makes no sense to fight. Why shouldn't i just say yes and be done with it. There is some consent; there is always some consent when one gets oneself into a situation like this. But it is not simply consent; this is too much. I am turning yes into lies. For instance,

this morning i got out of bed to make my own breakfast. I put on my robe, found the armholes. The effort nearly exhausted me and it was only inertia propelling me down the hall into the kitchen, but i got there. My visitor was standing by the stove frying four eggs. "Did you sleep well?" "Yes," i said. "Are you going to work today?" "Yes." "Then you'll need a good breakfast." He put eggs and toast and coffee down on the table in front of me.

See. I fooled him. I had no intention of working today. My only intention was to answer your letters. Thanks for writing. How are you?

Love, Lois

*

9 May

Dearest Lois,

Get the hell out of there. Here is a cheque for the first and last month's rent, enough for a three-bedroom apartment. Go out and get an apartment big enough for yourself and your kids.

I don't know who this visitor from hell is but obviously you have to get away. I'm not offering myself as an alternate rescuer, but as a friend with a few bucks to lend to you. I expect to be paid back. I will be coming down to Toronto in three weeks' time and we can discuss the lawsuit. I assume it concerns divorce and the custody of your children.

In the meantime, get out of that man's apartment as soon as you can. I will call you when I get into town.

Love, J.P.

*

May 16

Dear Jean-Philippe,

I've taken an apartment on Crawford near Queen, sandwiched between the artists and the psychiatric patients. This seems fine. The place was available for immediate occupancy so I occupied it immediately. The last tenant planted a thousand bulbs in my small garden that are all shooting green spears up from the ground. My phone will be installed tomorrow, so you can call Information for my new number. I got (thank God) my grant so I will be able to pay you back as soon as the money comes through. I'm looking forward to seeing you.

Thank you. How did you know?
Love, Lois

*

22 May

Dear Lois,

I knew you would be fine. Your use of punctuation suggested you were crazy but weren't yet mad, forgetting to capitalize the personal pronoun "I" while "he" was capitalized. At first I thought you had taken a mystic fit, and were referring to God while dissolving as the proper subject of your thought. *Keep that man the object.* You may be dealing with a real son-of-a-bitch, but obviously you were working this through, since you could write something. If I thought otherwise I would have come, but you are one to take care of yourself. As it is, since I can't come next week, I will call again.

Isn't this behaviour out of character for Michael? But I don't suppose you want to hear my opinion on that subject. Keep in touch.

Love, J.P.

*

June 1

Dear Jean-Philippe,

I picked up the receiver on the hunch that you'd be on the other end of the line and not my mother or, worse yet, Michael. Yes, thank you, I am better. Today I wrote something quite good and then I went out to buy a new dress. I intended to charge a blue silk number to my Visa account, but had reached my credit limit. Fine. It is best, I understand, to go into court flat broke.

I contacted your lawyer friend as you suggested. I suppose that is why Michael hasn't called; my lawyer has contacted him or, more likely, his lawyer. Michael won't be happy to hear what these people have to say. I wasn't either, but the discussion with one's lawyer concerning one's divorce proceedings isn't usually a happy occasion, I suppose. It is an odd process, don't you find, the disembodiment of a marriage as it becomes abstracted into so many issues outstanding with no direct contact when direct contact was the basis of the marriage, originally the only reason for the marriage, the touch, before

things spin off into other matters—children, property, money owed—issues pertaining to laws rather than to touch, so from now on everything is to be carried out through lawyers, his and hers. My one lawyer friend from several years ago complained to me that her marital disputes were much less civil than major business débâcles, although both are matters ironically designated Civil Law. It seemed that in her professional practice matrimony and acrimony were melding into a single phenomenon. Perhaps this should be a source of some hope, if people continue to feel stronger emotions with respect to their lovers than to their business transactions, but if I could hate my publisher rather than my husband I think I would be happier. In fact, if all our ambitions and neurotic suspicions could be channelled into our work so that our lovers were constantly rubbed and polished only by our nobler qualities . . .

surely we would starve to death; there would be incessant famine, which there is, of course, but I don't suppose that is the cause. We don't bifurcate our lives in this way. A man can't be jealous of his boss instead of his wife, nor can his wife be jealous her boss instead of her husband. Most likely they will be jealous of both the boss and the spouse, or they won't be jealous of anyone. Everything spills over into that which it is not. I realize this now that my marriage is over, or I assume it is over. Oddly enough, my lawyer is in a better position to verify this than am I, but many things are clearer to me now that I have my own apartment and have forced my life into a certain framework, creating a structure for my work and continued existence, having escaped the prison of my consent to the visitor. You are wrong about him, though, J.P. I'd slipped into his grammar, it's true, capitalizing his pronoun—a silly joke—because I read that in German they capitalize nouns and he is the only German noun I know. But as for him, he was only trying to help. It is clear to me now that he was acting with compassion but

why is that only clear to me now that it is not happening? Sometimes it is the other way around; something stops happening because it becomes clear to me what was happening, but what is happening now remains shrouded in near total darkness so that I am forced to grope, feeling my way like a blind person, without benefit of a seeing-eye dog or of a cane. I can get a cane. That is something I can do to help myself, and it will be both an antenna and a weapon. But I have mixed my metaphors; a shroud does not belong to a blind person but to someone who is dead and I am not dead but blind with rage and sadness, yet

doesn't a blind person develop a wonderful capacity to touch and to know by touching? Doesn't the object come alive beneath the fingers of her blind touch? And doesn't the object itself vibrate under the stroke of the blind lover whose hands are questioning in the constant night of her love? It happened

the way light is cast on the moon; while some surface is in shadow the crescent seems brighter, seems as bright as one's memory of its fullness, but one is not seeing as clearly and one is not seeing half the light ever or at all. Why is it that this inevitable ignorance never leaves me resigned, when neither the light I have nor that which is denied will suffice; it is still night. The tension that I sometimes call God is actually everything that exists between what we know and what we don't know, where anything is possible. I think in my whole life I've only ever been half in love, and at that only with what I didn't know,

excepting my children. I know my children. That's why I can accept Michael stealing them; since it isn't their fault or mine that they are gone, they will come back. I know. I know. And we will be fine, and there will be no blame between us. I'm sure I digress. I know you find this irritating and worrisome, but just one more thing—excepting you as well. There is this same quality of love between us, a love that makes no claim. And I presume to say this; maybe that is what's lost between you and Margaret. She mentions a cattle prod; I imagine a flagstaff a man plunges into a mountain he's climbed and thinks he can claim. You can name but not claim a mountain. What does it mean to own a mountain, after all, except that you can use it for a time, mine it. But it is different between you and me, and as close I think as a man and woman can get to Jesus' love or, ideally, a lesbian's love. No claim is made, just love and liberty held in perfect balance; we both do with it what we want. Then anything is possible,

but to return to the earlier subject, what happened last month —the visitor, being Michael's colleague, was privy to information regarding Michael's plans to remain in England. Now I realize that the reason we were mere acquaintances was because Michael loathed him. "He is so damn transparent," Michael sneered, as if being thick and opaque are primary virtues. This seems to be Michael's point of view but what I know is that only angels are transparent

so when this visitor came to see how I was handling matters, in my despair I recognized him as an angel of mercy and I let him serve me. It is fine that it happened and fine that it is not happening now (with the help of your thoughtful intervention, but withdraw the invectives) and yes

Michael is suing for divorce. He has basically stolen the

children which doesn't surprise me nor does it worry me. The children were bound to find him out sooner or later; far better that they learn because he demonstrates who he is. If it had been otherwise I might have had to tell them someday and these are not words a mother tells her children; better he shows them who he is and how he is. What surprises me is my calm about them. At first, it is true, I panicked, but that has passed. Now I am going to write something important,

something about photographs of Eritrea, knowing full well that this project will be a failure. Frances also knows this. She doesn't believe in the project, knows that the last famine made history but now famine and war are not historical because no one cares to record them, least of all me. The news now is peace and its resulting chaos.

Last night I crawled into a neighbourhood restaurant, the kind with three-dimensional paintings hanging on the wall depicting rivers that actually shimmer if the painting is plugged in. I ordered a western on brown bread with a side of fries, and it was a relief to know this is what the waitress would deliver. Waitressing is the application of the law of supply and demand in its most pure form. A waitress knows what to deliver because this is what the customer asks for; there is always some mutual satisfaction. Nothing I do is like this. My productivity, if one can even refer to writing or mothering as something that results in a product, answers no specific need. It is essentially superfluous. At its best. At its worst it's reactionary, an answer to some need or moralistic outcry, and that is simply bad art. You sound distracted,

you allude to a problem that I hope is not more weighty than Margaret's increased poundage, but I want to respect your privacy. You'll discuss it with me, no doubt, if and when you feel it may be useful or cathartic. I always like what Robert Frost said about this, that two people who don't love can't be together without having things about which they don't speak, just as two people who do love each other can't have matters about which they won't speak. Mind you, he was referring to a married couple who had lost their only child. Our situation is quite different but

I must tell you, Jean, I had a lovely dream of you and Margaret living in a wonderful home. The first floor for daily living was all openings and no doors, the living room with its grand piano and luminous blue painting on the wall like sky in its different seasons, and a dining table set for your supper, the space a perfect balance of sound, light, scents and tastes. Your office and library were on the second floor with books lining the walls floor to ceiling. But not to the ceiling; this was the most lovely thing, the ceiling vaulting up above your office to a loft, private but connected with skylights. There must have been a children's room beneath the loft but it was out of view. The loft floor was covered with carpets and strewn with cushions. A pivoting mirror in an oak frame reflected Margaret's body, round large breasts above a pregnant abdomen, as she lay on a bed laden with duvets, lace and pastel colours. (I realize it's none of my business, J.P., but have you two ever considered children?) I'd like to hold onto this dream for myself, J.P., but I think it belongs to you and had merely been mislaid in the dark.

Love, Lois

*

10 June

Lois dear,

Are you illiterate? You suggest a baby, for God's sake? When Margaret's and my body join we are each left with half a life rather than a third. Multiplication is impossible. At best we can accomplish an uneasy equilibrium, a certain weight maintained between us, now her gaining, me losing. Look, tomorrow I will go back to work, and then the next day I will work and then the next day I will work again and the pattern will be my release.

I know, however, what would be a release: war. Don't give me peace. It's idiocy, with more weaponry poised than ever. Why is there no war, no release from this terrible tension? If there was a war everything else would be beside the point except my body because bodies are what count in a war, the body count.

This is beyond your comprehension which is perhaps my own fault. I can't express this ennui. It is not anxiety attached to a misconstrued past or to an uncertain future, nor an ambience of anxiety arising out of the present circumstances. There is a shifting in the ground beneath me that I cannot express either, and in any case, comprehension demands an *a priori* sympathy. It is a precondition for understanding, not a result that can be spun wholly new from antipathy and incomprehension. Therefore, when you fail to understand, and if I understand that your misunderstanding is due to the magnitude of your own pressing problems, then my frustration is compounded; I become doubly understanding while you remain uncomprehending. We can only change the subject. The doorbell is ringing, no doubt the pizza Margaret ordered.

Avec amitié, J.P.

*

June 14

Please, Jean-Philippe,

don't wish for a war. I'm writing about famine and now you—

a war. What we imagine too often occurs; this is too much; this could spin out of control,

I am afraid. The other day an old man from the hospital sat down next to me on a bench in the park, turned to me squinting his eyes and asked why I was frightened. I'm not frightened, I told him. Oh, but you are, he told me. Have faith, he said. Faith clears the cobwebs from the mind. Faith even does away with the spiders. I'm feeding the birds, I told him. Ah, you have the time, he said. Listen. Then he told me about a plague of spiders in his parents' summer home where he spent his holidays as a child. He was terrified of these bugs, and although his teachers scolded him and his peers taunted him, so much more threatening were these creatures that he began to dread the end of the school term. One night in abject horror, one week before summer break, he promised God he would always believe if God would just get rid of the spiders. All these years, and the old man had never seen another spider. He rummaged through his pocket, and produced a pamphlet, worn and folded, with scripture passages illustrating various human conditions. He couldn't read the words despite his thick glasses, and I wondered if he'd induced blindness to avoid seeing spiders, to preserve his faith. And what if I formulated a similar prayer, to end my famine, to prevent your war

or simply to eliminate spiders in my home. Probably the entire region would suffer an extraordinary blight of spiders. The trees would be draped with webs and we'd trip as the threads wound themselves around our ankles. No,

I could imagine the spiders extinct and they would be extinct, just as this madman has done, but I don't enjoy the way we can manipulate reality with our imaginations. Real things should resist, should remain just what they are despite our idea of them. Even when things change, the change ought to be part of what the thing is and relate only tangentially to our idea of it, our articulations. Objects are supposed to be objective and I disdain the flexibility of the imagination, the abstraction of words and sentences that I can arrange any way I want. Sometimes I'm surprised when a story ends tidily, having forgotten that I'd planned that it would end tidily from the outset. The aesthetic makes its own demands, and an internal order to the fiction demands its own resolution, but it is and remains my aesthetic, my fiction, subject to my distortions. It's more shocking yet when this happens in lived life. Choice brings the world closer, inevitable, beginning with what we imagine, and it makes me so anxious. For God's sake, J.P., don't wish for a war.

Love, Lois

*

21 June

"Dear Lois," Jean-Philippe writes patiently. "I think I do understand. Yes, of course I do, but my understanding is irrelevant. It is your self-absorption which leaves me beyond your comprehension, reduces this correspondence to diarizing, and if this doesn't change I will save postage and keep a journal."

"Oh," Jean-Philippe imagines Lois to be thinking. "I beg your pardon. How is your work going? Are you nearly finished your translation? And how is your health? I do hope you've put on some weight, that Margaret has lost some weight, and that this has relieved your sexual tension. Are you getting along swimmingly and is your book almost complete?"

"The book is almost done. It should be done within the next few months," Jean-Philippe replies, skirting the other issues Lois just raised.

"I'm so happy for you."

"And how is your book coming? Weren't you about to write something fairly specific about famine in Eritrea and then move on to another chapter?" Jean-Philippe politely enquires.

Yes he does.

Love, J.P.

*

June 25

Dear Jean-Philippe,

Michael is sending the children home within a month's time! I'm going to fix up their rooms, paint their walls, have everything ready. I've sent paint samples so they can choose their colours. I unpacked the boxes containing their toys, threw stuffed animals on the floor so it looks the way it always did, as if they were home already. I hung crystals in the basement window in Diane's room to spew rainbows on her walls with the late-afternoon sun. Daniel will be ten by the time he comes home, Diane twelve, perhaps too old for summer camp, do you think? They've always gone before and I'll ask if they want to go but hope they say no. I want to spend August with them. We can laze around Harbourfront, listen to music and watch the boats. We can go to the plays at High Park. Daniel loves fishing there even if we can't eat what he catches; he just wants to watch their scales shimmer in his palm before he lets them go. I hope they like our new apartment. I hope to have the manuscript completed before they arrive; that's my goal. It was proceeding slowly, making daily life almost impossible. Last week I was sitting in my room and realized that the front porch light was left on. I got up to turn it off, concerned about wasting electricity, but then realized that getting up, crossing the room, flicking the switch expends energy as well. The arithmetic was too much for me. I didn't know what to do, and paralysis would have set in if I pondered the penultimate question: am I a waste of energy, the source of some hunger in the web of choices? But now I must get on with it; the children are coming.

And how are you?

Love, Lois

*

July 6

Dear J.P.

The rabbit died. Literally. (God, I used to laugh at the expression; now I see it for what it is. Killing a rabbit to confirm a woman's pregnancy is sacrificial substitution, a death for a life. The rabbit has nothing to do with it. We kill it

so there's not too much life, and it must be a rabbit, symbol of sensuality and pleasure. Isn't caging it enough?) Now my rabbit is dead. You remember Bunstable? Now she is dead. It happened like this, this morning:

she caught a virus. Last night she had diarrhoea. I noticed but sometimes it's caused merely by a change of diet or the weather. I kept her warm, gave her plenty of fresh water. That is what one is supposed to do and that is just what I did

and this morning she seemed better. The papers I'd spread were clean. Now I realize that the diarrhoea stopped because she was dehydrated, but I thought then it meant she was better. I picked her up and her breathing was laboured. It was so sad. I called the vet. The office is closed on Saturdays. I called another. The same thing. And another. By now I was weeping, holding her and speaking softly so she could hear and not be frightened. I told her she had to be here when the children came back. We need her to receive our love. I thought talking like this would work, that she'd understand and buck up, but just then she died. In my arms. I sighed, then take our love to God.

I've never felt so defeated in my life. She just quit. Life went out of her. Gave up the ghost. This is exactly the way it is. The words we use are completely accurate. If we talk about birth or sex the words are often wrong but when it comes to death we've got it exactly right. Isn't that terrible to think about? I've been wailing for hours and can barely pick out the keys to write to you. What do I tell the children?

Love, Lois.

*

July 12

Dear Jean-Philippe

I received Pierre Jahan and Cocteau's book. Thank you. It is quite close to the style I have in mind for this project, a spare text tangential to the photographs with its own integrity as written language, unlike many such texts, and I've pored over many. I am not an idiot; I look for help, or at least condolence, where it might be found and I usually find it in a library. But this particular grope for friends-among-coffee-table-book-writers proved disappointing. Our leading literary lioness, for instance, wrote a text for a photo essay on Nature (capitalized and female) in which poets and photographers are referred to as male (he, not capitalized) although this poet and this photographer are both women. No one holds the text against her; it's not commented upon in critical essays about her work. No one, I suppose, reads such texts, unless they're trying to write one themselves, so the writer safely abandons consciousness to get down to this literary housework, something one must do for the money or for a friend. Why can't I do that? Clearly the photographic images eclipse consciousness—I can *see* that now—and lack of consciousness allows the unconscious truth to rise up, which might be these texts' single virtue. Take John le Carré's extraordinary introduction to Don McCullin's *Heart of Darkness*. Le Carré is crazy about his subject, draws our attention to McCullin's hands: "you would know at once that he punches with both hands. He is dreadfully vulnerable.... He doesn't trust: he's wide open, waiting to be screwed." Their entire encounter is described in terms of sexual battle. Le Carré learns that McCullin never shoots (not snaps; children snap photos while men shoot) without taking a light-reading. "Christ, I thought," (le Carré), "remembering some of those photographs. Thinking of Hué and the Khe Sanh and the Tet offensive and other impenetrable hells where I have not been, but where everything I have heard tells me there is no incentive to take any kind of reading whatever; where the only serious incentive was to hold your balls and pray and stay alive." What does a woman hold, I wondered, and looked at McCullin's photos to find this out. According to the photos, women are often holding a baby or a dead body, sometimes a baby's dead body. Actually, the men are often holding babies or a dead or dying body, sometimes a baby's dead body and McCullin is obviously holding his camera; no one is holding balls. But le Carré doesn't seem to see that, and if seeing is all one can do with photos and we can't do that either, then perhaps they make us stupid. I took out William's photos again. Examining them,

my attention shifted away from the photos as sources of data and I focused on them as aesthetic objects, confounding objectivity. I recognized my physical response, that I find them exceedingly beautiful. Each image, framed by the perimeters of the lens and film, is composed, the composure of a shoot of grain in the expanding desert as intriguing as a starving child and I am back to the subject of the photo, at a loss with the aesthetic, with myself as subject. Perhaps you're relieved, supposing I will now get down to writing something on the subject of famine in Eritrea, and move on to the next chapter. No. If I ignore myself as seeing subject and remain subjected to this flood of images, I won't write (com)passionately or see these objects (com)passionately. In time I won't even be able to read, my capacity for compassion so eroded. I'll feel nothing. But it's not a conspiracy, this aesthetic failure, not a conspiracy to make the unhungry stupid and the hungry dead, but an underlying logic to the world as we've created it, in our own image, half stupid and half dead,

half banal and half tragic. We've split the earth's hemispheres along these fault lines, but already the logic is unravelling. I am in the wealthy hemisphere but so thin now it hurts to be touched. In the banal hemisphere my mother calls and asks what I've been doing and I explain why I'm making field trips to hungry people, to food banks, the Scott Mission and Nellie's, a women's shelter. "Oh yes, it happens here," my mother tells me. "We've discussed it in our church, but it's not always anyone's fault. You yourself almost starved as a baby." She explained how she'd some problem nursing me and when the doctor noted on his chart that I wasn't gaining weight he had her give me formulas to which I proved allergic, and then the whole business became rather desperate. Babies' allergies back then—who had even heard of such a thing? Mother asks. Then she says that, thank heaven, this wouldn't happen to a mother nowadays because all mothers nurse their babies and doctors know everything about allergies. This is the good thing about women's lib, which is how my mother still refers to feminism, having read a bit about it in magazines. There are more women doctors, who naturally understand all about babies and nursing, she says, so that even if such a thing did happen to a woman now she could go to one of these wonderful women doctors, so it's very unlikely to happen, what happened to her

(and to me as well, although she didn't say that. After first mentioning the fact that it was me who almost starved, she told the story as if it were hers alone and I were simply the listener, as if I couldn't possibly know this baby because it all happened back then. This manner of speaking that we fall into with children confuses me)

but the information, however banal, proves helpful. I can start to unravel the logic imposed on me by the existence of these photos and vocabulary. I must have some knowledge of my subject and it is my body's knowledge, dimly recalled. I might be able to write about hunger and not be, as they say, beside myself. I think I might be able to settle down soon to write, like you, to find release through my work

(or I presume you are released. I'm only guessing. I haven't heard from you in almost a month. It proves convenient that we have the same editor and that she is such a gossip. She told me she received your draft. Are you eating now,

and also, was food taken across the barricades for the people at Oka yet? I saw pictures—why are there always pictures taken and nothing offered? What do you think about this business?)

Love, Lois

*

July 19

Dear Jean-Philippe,

Still no letter. I want to come visit you before the children arrive. I've tried to call. Has Margaret failed to give you my messages? I think this morning she hung up on me. Please call me or at least write and say whether this is an appropriate time for me to visit.

Love, Lois

July 27

Dear Jean-Philippe,

perhaps seeing is believing after all. It was necessary and I'm glad I visited even if it strained us all. Now I can see. Any fool could see. What are you going to do? Margaret looks ill; you don't need me to tell you that and of course you must try to persuade her to go back to her doctor. This weight gain cannot be healthy, but I am more alarmed by your weight loss. Being ten pounds underweight is more detrimental to one's health than being twenty pounds overweight, although it would seem that problem is more nearly twenty pounds under, forty pounds over. I will say no more. You are quite correct;

this is none of my business unless you choose to make it my business, a cutting but honest remark. I should indeed relegate the whole issue to that which is "out there" which I know nothing about, which is none of my business but

I see now, I have been a bad friend, first to ignore, then to intrude, but what was I to do? Was it wrong to witness the way you two are carving up the space between you? This is an appalling example of body sculpture, and perhaps you need a critic to say so. Please write and tell me you forgive me.

Love, Lois

*

30 July

Dear Lois,

　　Margaret is pregnant. She is throwing me out. Don't

contact me here. I'll write soon.

    J.P.

*

                                          August 3

Dear Jean-Philippe,

really? how awful,

and now also there may be a war in the Gulf.

The children arrive tomorrow and I am in bedlam trying to get things ready. Still, I tried to call, to congratulate you and Margaret. Congratulations (I guess).

Love to you both, Lois

*

                                            16 August

Dear Lois,

    I told you not to write, to mind your own business, but that aside, I'm here now, in the apartment of the girl hereafter referred to as the nymph of Foufounes' pool table. One terrible afternoon—was it just three days ago?—Margaret arrived back at our apartment, hereafter referred to as her apartment, with a large sack of maternity clothes. She'd purchased special nursing bras with snaps to expose her breasts, pants with elastic front panels resembling belly slings for an expanding abdomen, shirts like tents and enormous sweaters. She set these items out on the bed, staring down at them and then at me staring down at them from the bedroom doorway, and she asked me to leave. I moved towards the kitchen to get a coffee, and she followed, saying, "No, I mean leave the apartment. Permanently." "But we're having a baby," I protested and she retorted, "How do you even know it's yours?"

Well, I know. Who else would have the courage to sleep with this dragon? No one but I and even my energies were flagging. I was tired of wrestling with her. I packed a small bag, descended to my depth at a table at Foufounes where I sat watching the bubbles in my beer rise; I was drowning in that pitcher, and she found me there. Now the nymph is curled up next to me in her bed, hereafter referred to as our bed. She is a pharmacology student at the University of Montreal, as happy to have a roomie as I am to have a room. Her English is poor and she can't make out my scribble. She is under the impression that Lois is an Englishman's name.

I suppose you think I am an utter cad to leave my pregnant wife stranded while I curl up in a nymph's nest across town, but Margaret told me to get out so I did. This apartment is a soft space, billowing roman blinds and pillows, a coral garden of colour, shade and light. I've never felt more at home. She is lying next to me with her hair tied up and when I loosen the scarf a light brown wave sweeps over my face. Her lips are cool as a fish. When I first saw her at the bar I thought only of birds, her long neck stretched like a swan's, but here everything is watery. She wears t-shirts when she gets out of bed and her tight young ass beneath the shirt shines small crescent moons when I look up. I think about your visitor to whom you could only answer "yes". I too can only express assent but there is a difference; I can accept this bliss. You and I are different after all. Don't send me a cheque for two months' rent; I don't want to escape.

You may write me here or might choose not to write a rogue in which case this is the place to which you are not writing. We are situated near the corner of Côte-des-Neiges and Queen Mary in the shadow of St. Joseph's Oratory, convenient for the nymph because it is close to the university and convenient for me because there is a mountain between Margaret and myself. Tomorrow I'm climbing up to the oratory to pray to Brother André that Margaret miscarries, and if my prayer is answered I'll hang a pair of her maternity pants up among the crutches in the shrine. Be well.

    Sincerely, J.P.

*

August 21

Dear Jean-Philippe,

I wouldn't say you're cad; I don't know what to think. There is too much context, which is very much like not enough context insofar as judgement dies, either by drowning or starvation, don't you think? I would like to know the woman's name since I can't possibly refer to her as you do, as the nymph. That is all. I apologize if that is too much to ask, if I'm intruding.

The children arrived two weeks ago and we settled into a happy routine of short outings, fast food and visiting with friends right up until they set off for camp. Camp was their choice. There has been so much change they wanted something the same. Camp is always the same, and I can get down to work. I wanted to be finished the project by now, but I hadn't which is fortunate because I've had another thought entirely on how best to proceed and this is it:

sentences are constructions while words are mere sounds of opposing energy, that might blow up as atoms do, if you hit them hard enough

and this is similar to images, to photographs. I have been trying to make sense of William's images, using my words to construct a sentence, that string of pearls, each pearl layer upon layer of dried oyster saliva, each string a cliché,

a series of words, a grammatical order, one complete thought consisting of a subject and a verb, either of which may be understood and therefore omitted from the actual sentence although both remain an intrinsic part of the sentence's logic.

In music a sentence is also one complete thought, three or four phrases, but

a sentence can also be an opinion or a judgement that follows some deliberation, as in the legal context, the conclusion of some authority, that of either a judge or a tribunal (and is this the overlap with the literary meaning, author being the authority?), and we use the odd expression that a sentence is passed, as if it must be accepted the way a grammatical sentence comes to be received in either music or literature, which depends upon the reader's or listener's receptivity. Certainly a sentence doesn't depend on the criminal's receptivity. There is no such requirement. This is confusing, and I don't want the reader to feel sentenced, but

how can I create a context, beginning with William's photos and my jangle of words, that might produce a resonance, a climate of receptivity, when virtually every subject of William's art is dead and the present context of the photo is my living room? Any other context I create is pure fiction, and I refuse to create a context more satisfying than that which is a given, when the Eritreans' hunger is not satisfied. I have an idea, but

it is not what Frances has in mind. She wants me to expand upon a proposition, something like "war is hell" or "famine is quite bad for one's health." Now I understand why non-fiction books take shape as book proposals; they are shaped by propositions that might be more fictitious than anything set out in a book of fiction. Fiction is at least shaped by the principles of its own aesthetics that tends to be wily as hell and difficult to sell, but

speaking of Frances, she asked me if I had your address because there are some minor problems with the translations you sent her. She wants to discuss it with you and doesn't know where you are presently residing. Not wanting to presume your intentions, I didn't give her your new address but I will do so if you instruct me to, or you might write to her directly.

Yours sincerely, Lois

*

30 August

Dear Lois,

Someday you must read our correspondence in sequence, witness yourself your total preoccupation with yourself that excludes everything apart from your own thinking process, if indeed it constitutes a process and not a nearly impenetrable cloud of unknowing. My God, Lois, I'm curled up to a stranger's body when my wife is expecting a baby in fives months' time and all you want to know is my lover's name. It's Charlotte. She's going out now to pick up some souvlaki. What am I doing here?

It's hot. The late afternoon is full of moisture. If I move at all I feel as if I'm swimming and this is not the sea after all but a tub of dirty water, and if Charlotte pulls the stopper all my energy will swirl down the drain, perhaps my whole body. I have no energy reserved; it's all dissolved and subject to the maelstrom.

Yesterday I went downtown and suddenly I was surrounded

by cops carrying rifles, not over their shoulders but poised, ready to shoot. It had something to do with the Mohawk stand-off—I figured that out later—but at first the police were staring at me, confused, and I stood before them, my hands above my head, convicted.

A distant authority informs me that I am going to be a father. The assertion, not conception, the claim a woman makes rather than the sexual act, establishes paternity. Perhaps there were children before but, without the assertion, I didn't become a father. Sex and procreation, existentially speaking, are just coincidentally related. In fact, they are opposite: sex reminds us of our birth, children of our death.

I must consider what I am going to do here. Charlotte is very young, for which there's no cure other than time and I don't have as much as she does. She's in a flap about her waitressing job which she can't afford to quit although her school year begins next week. She doesn't eat properly, and I am forced to fix proper meals. I'm regaining the weight I lost, a bit of belly hangs down like a hammock when I bend over to pick up Charlotte's soiled stockings that she leaves strewn on the floor. An hour after she's left for work, once I've washed up, put the place back in order, perhaps prepared and refrigerated a casserole for dinner, I sit down and consider what I'm going to do. I'm going to be a father in the new year and my wife, the mother of my baby, doesn't want to see me again.

Now, only in my memory and far too late, I can see Margaret in her proper dimensions. As I packed my bag the afternoon she threw me out, she stood in the doorway. She is short, five foot four, slightly overweight but principally enlarged with the pregnancy, an acceptable weight, her energy sufficient. I thought she might cry, but she looked on with a curious near-smile as if she was seeing something pretty, perhaps a shaft of light against the wall behind me because she wasn't looking directly at me. She is not the alligator in Jean

Cocteau's bad dream after all. My anger turned on itself and I was the dragon swallowing my own tail. With my mouth full, I couldn't speak. I headed for the door and she stayed behind in the kitchen doorway. I expected her to turn around and . . . what? to blow me a kiss? She did not turn around.

Do you think you might speak to Margaret? Tell her I want to talk with her. Tell her I'm willing to work something out, and even if we can't work anything out between ourselves, we still have to work out a suitable arrangement for the baby. She doesn't answer her phone. I leave messages she never answers. Come to think of it, I don't know how you might reach her unless you made another trip to Montreal and that's too much to ask. Have you any suggestions about what I should do? Now there's someone knocking at the door. It's Charlotte. She's forgotten her keys.

Love, J.P.

*

September 10

Dear Jean-Philippe,

It wasn't too much to ask and I would have come to Montreal but Margaret's phone has been disconnected and there's no new listing. I can only assume she moved. Were you aware of this? I tried to contact a few mutual friends, but the only two people I could reach have heard from neither Margaret nor you recently, and I didn't want to contact Margaret's mother here in Toronto, afraid that would be indiscreet.

I pulled out Cocteau's book that you'd sent to examine the reference you made. I see. I am not indifferent to your predicament. I don't offer any advice because I am sure you will do the right thing, and I really have no idea what that is.

Cocteau writes,
"Le métier de poète, métier qui ne s'apprend pas, consiste à placer les objets du monde visible, devenus invisible par la gamme de l'habitude, dans une position insolite qui frappe le regard de l'âme et leur donne de la tragédie."

Cocteau, Jahan, the sculpture, the workmen who were ordered to heave the sculptures onto the scrap heap, the administrators who issued the order, are engaged in a war of realities and clearly each one makes a claim

as I must make a claim. The possibility of war makes me crazy. I went to a demonstration at the American Embassy. I've written the prime minister. There is nothing more to be done: they are transfixed with the logic, as were you. There will be a war and there will be more famine. But my children are back in school. My day has an imposed structure so I can get back to work. The writer approaches her subject,

but surely this is a misnomer. The writer is the subject and in this instance William's photos are the object while the subjects of the photos, famine's victims, are the indirect objects in this grammar, or are relegated to prepositional phrases. I received this structure as language itself is received, as an inheritance, a weight. I can create a certain balance or break it up, heap prepositional phrases upon phrases until the object and subject are confounded, which is precisely what I intend to do

but this is a limited freedom. The grammar reinstates its own logic and a book is only what it is. The people in the photos are still seriously reduced in size, and it is impossible to frame another's reference, so

what can I do? Is there any way I can be of assistance to you?

Love, Lois

*

19 September

Dear Lois,

Thank you for what you might have done. It's a rare woman who makes no claim on some *a priori* female knowledge or moral insight. I admire you. I curse you, you bitch. I'm left bereft of an imposed direction, a system of moral argument that I was led to believe would be provided to me as my birthright, and my freedom rises like a great bear in front of me and hesitates to attack, looms over me because I crouch.

I finally explained to Charlotte in some detail my predicament and predictably she took a fit of feminist rage, railing against men in general and me in particular in such precise language I was momentarily rendered speechless. This, as you know, is unusual. I think perhaps I deserve it. I have behaved like a fool, a total idiot, worse than shit, as she informed me. Still, only when I say it aloud or when Charlotte snarls at me, "Réveille-toi, tu vas avoir un enfant d'elle, trou-du-cul," does the simple biological fact of paternity make its way into my consciousness.

Fatherhood is not a straightforward idea for me. It has the quality of a doctrine, a received truth rather than an objective reality, and what do I know about it? Practically nothing, which always suited me fine. I think about my own father. He was the stranger who sat across from me at breakfast, eating oatmeal and drinking coffee. "Good morning, son," he'd say to me every morning. I slid into the pressed-back chair across from him. I'd watch him fastidiously stir one teaspoon of sugar and one pat of butter into his porridge. Thank God he drank his coffee black or breakfast might have taken all day. I'd spoon heaping tablespoons of brown sugar into my porridge and watch the butter melt and swirl as I stirred. "Don't mess with your food," he sometimes added to "Good morning, son." That was Father.

Of course, I have other associations, the god-like father, our Father, the collective *our*, the symbolic *Father*, who art in heaven, out of harm's way so long as he stays up there. Margaret is right; I should stay out of my child's way. We gave up too much when we gave up the Galilean universe. Knowing that time moves backwards beyond the speed of light and that space curves inward, Father threatens to come too close.

It comes down to practical matters. I must decide what I'm going to do, then find Margaret and negotiate. Charlotte will not impede me in any way, or offer suggestions. She has stepped aside. I think she is already seeing someone new, someone her own age, someone she can hope to understand. I fix her breakfast and she's too tired to eat. She has lunch at the university. Last night I went out of my way to prepare her favourite pasta sauce, but she was too much in a hurry to eat it, planning to go out to the cinema. I watched her putting on her makeup, leaning over the dresser to study her pores in the mirror and powder her face. I watched her unscrew pots of pastel colours and blend them over her eyes, dust her cheeks. She was making her face pretty for someone else and I was obsessed with the specifics of the procedure. In the end I stormed and made a sufficient fuss that she was dissuaded from leaving. She obediently ate her dinner, then curled up next to me on the bed. In the morning nothing had changed. I still must decide what I must do *qua* father, given the perimeters Margaret has drawn, and it will take me away from Charlotte. She is not the mother but a child. I am not a child but a father. These aren't random points.

Even though Charlotte is gone most of the time, her tasteful interior decoration affords me some comfort, softening the blow of introspection. Outside is a desert. The neighbourhood offers nothing, unremitting privacy, rows and rows of apartment buildings, public places that aren't open past nine. The bagel shop and restaurants are nearly empty by then. Here night is our own responsibility, everyone inside with their private happiness or agony, it hardly matters which, the privacy itself being everything. There's no escaping the job of taking stock; I'd nearly averted it by taking a young lover, just to find it imposed by geography.

  I think I will have to go back to Toronto, at least for a few days, to see if I can locate Margaret. Sister of Mercy, Daughter of Perpetual Motion, Mother Lois with Eyes Like Knives, can I visit you? I am lonely and Charlotte is too young; she can't console me properly. I miss you.

  Avec amitié, J.P.

*

September 27

Dear Jean-Philippe,

certainly you can visit and stay here if you wish. We are friends and that is always in the present tense, present to each other, tense, but for God's sake, it's September. I always get depressed in September, as if I take the fall literally and do. Still, I will try to be a friend. Still,

I think we are too obsessed with the ways the past comes to inhabit the present. For instance, you are not your father or any prior reflection of fatherliness. We must begin to explore how the present inhabits the present (which means, for myself, while I write this I try to locate the words present in my own body. With this letter the words have settled into my fingers and it is easy. The words of the Eritrean text rest in my intestine for the moment, ingestion, appropriating the material, some to be transformed into energy, work, and the rest to be shat and flushed) but

I also want to consider more carefully how the future comes to inhabit the present. The present mirrors one's idea of the future in the realm of our choices. This is too seldom explained to young girls. Certainly it strikes me as new as I think about it. I considered how our apocalyptic imaginations affect our present reality, beckon us to make good our worst dreams, to make quite specific choices. But when did we embrace hunger? Does our Judeo-Christian metaphor of desert travel lead to desertification? does our idea that some are damned damn some? and are our dreams of death seeds planted in the present moment? When I examine William's photos I must acknowledge that they are beautiful, resonate with something I've already accepted as lovely, a germ of an idea, a dream. Is hunger our black bride skulking in Africa, starving? Our racism reinforces our rapture; these are wedding photos, nudes, erotic pietàs, a body languishing before the groom's and her own mother's proud eyes, before our eyes, and we are ravished. The past, present and future move outside of time, famine intimating eternal divine love,

but according to *Time-Life* famine is not a great theme in photography. The grand themes are the human condition, the nature of death, the portrait, the nude, nature and war, and early in this project I attempted to organize William's photos within such a determined structure, the common sense that these coffee-table books represent, and what is more common than hunger? I suppose William's photos resemble war, but I don't want to participate in expanding the metaphor for war, even a war against hunger. Let war end, first in our imaginations so it may end in our lives. Categories confound me. I look again at the photos. What order might these photographic subjects impose? And what in turn do their subjects want? Not another photo. Obviously the actual people want some order that includes the provision of food, and after that more food, and then a way to produce food so after today they can have food, and after tomorrow food, and then the next day, food. That's all but as this order plays over as a mantra to reach the heart of the matter, I think: desire is actually contra-progress. My words for desire are all repetitive, rhythmic, not textual, stomach rumblings, a groan of lust,

while most sentences are constructed with subject, a verb and a direct object. Someone must do something to someone or something according to our grammatical tastes. The simple subject/verb is unsatisfying, if something just is, just acts. I long for this simpler grammar, a subject and its complement, or simply a phrase that isn't prepositional. Can one write such a book?

Not I. I am sentenced while I dream of parole. Speech. Words committed to the air and, if written, as tone is to a musical score. Anyone who hears wants to dance

but no one is going to dance to this text about hunger. I was mistaken at the outset. Hunger is not intense desire; it is thwarted desire. William is a concerned photographer. He wants me to experience these people's hunger. Yet, if I experience anything at all it is not in my stomach but in my neck, stretching to see more, but more what? not more photos. Is the desire this stretching in my neck? Is it the beginning of a dance? I am hopelessly confused about my choices here

but nevertheless, you are welcome to stay.

Love, Lois

*

5 October

Dear Lois,

If there's any truth to what you write, our dreams create

the present rather selectively. For instance, you dreamt a happy future for Margaret and me. I, on the other hand, dreamt of a ferocious dragon eating its own tail, doomed. It was a terrifying nightmare, Lois, and I woke up in cold wet sheets, having soaked the bedding with my sweat and fear. Cocteau wrote in the book that I sent you, the one with Pierre Jahan's photographs, "Cet homme politique en redingote, cet alligator se sont rencontrés dans le mauvais rêve d'un poète." The alligators in the photo were melted down to scrap metal for Hitler's monuments, bent, twisted, eating their own tails.

Meanwhile, Margaret has left town, not simply fat but pregnant, as my life comes undone. My objection does not pertain to what you say or see, but to what you fail to say or see in all this.

Your pun on the word *sentence* is peculiar to English. In French we refer to a sentence as *une phrase*; so there's no such confusion. You see, language is more plastic than you imagine. Most of us use it as if it is, at any rate. Consider its utility. Take an old friend of mine. Yesterday we had lunch at his favourite Chinese restaurant, where he surprised me by speaking fluent Chinese with the waiter and then the proprietor, who visited our table briefly. When did you learn Chinese? I enquired after they'd gone to the kitchen. My friend explained that he taught himself Chinese so he could get the best Chinese food in town and it worked; certainly we were served a tremendous spread. This same man learned French so he could do business here, Chinese to eat, Hebrew to pray and continued to carry on most of his daily life in English, his mother tongue. Is this a problem? He seems content. Lois, be happy.

In any case, I don't really have time to make a trip to Toronto right now. I want to get down to some new writing. I finished the translation, received the rest of my advance and now can begin this murder mystery, to hell with everything else. Charlotte is taking terrible care of herself. I make her favourite cakes and casseroles, which she refuses, so I consume them. She's taken a new lover. Yesterday she showed me the earrings he gave her. "What the hell is this about?" I protested. She feigned surprise. "I can't be unfaithful to you when we never wanted to be faithful. That is impossible." In addition to her pharmacology courses, apparently she's studying logic. I want a lobotomy.

    Sincerely, J.P.

*

October 17

Jean-Philippe,

be happy you say? Yesterday was Michael's and my anniversary but I remembered too late, only today after I'd ruined everything. Anniversaries rebound on me. I don't remember them, but the anniversary comes and if it was a happy day, on its anniversary I celebrate, not remembering what I celebrate, but I must dimly remember and whatever is remembered still exists, is re-created so that perhaps all creating is remembering, re-creating a comfortable reiteration of what was, is, will be again, repetitive as a mantra, a prayer

which is no comfort to me, not today, and what the hell do I care if it is a comfort for some when it isn't for me since yesterday was the anniversary of a disaster, and if the day is the anniversary of a disaster I create havoc all around me even years later and my stunned children conclude that I am mad. I am not mad but live in spirally time, unconscious of the turning of the screw

so that yesterday all that moved from memory into consciousness was a sensation of falling. I thought, this is love; I am falling in love. And thinking God who is constant would catch me, I decided to meet my visitor for lunch and he agreed. I was falling and looking up when I noticed that my visitor's lips were moving. I had finished my salad and he was sipping his soup and I could not understand what he was saying, at first thinking he was speaking his German as I was trying to speak my mother's tongue, the language of love, but he was calling into the abyss into which I'd fallen so there was the echo also to contend with, yet I recognized some of his words though his voice seemed to pile up on itself. Utterly confused,

trying to summarize the point he was making, to check if this was in fact what he was saying, which at first I might have missed, having simply brushed against the point as a cat brushes against a leg as she heads for her food dish (this being before God lost its balance and I was dropped to the bottom), I said:

you mean you want us to be lovers but you don't want anything to change because of the implications of your desire, but what about my uterus where I might receive your love; it might get bigger instead of smaller—oh, we should be careful—yes—and if I remain small, become even smaller, your desire might shrink accordingly.

I could tell by his expression, irritation mixed with relief, that I'd pretty well hit the mark dead on. This is when, I think, God slipped, and I knew I couldn't trust my instincts when I was feeling so low. I had to formulate all possible options, to set them out succinctly and choose among them.

One: I would forget this lunch happened, go home, make the children's supper and go to bed. This option had the advantage of being a familiar response, assuaging his fears that something might happen, and I would have got some much-needed sleep.

Two: I could have told him to go to hell which would have converted this scenario into a scene with decisive conflict, sides drawn; it would have led to a denouement. In a scene I could have been creative, sought resolution, but it required a certain quality of galvanized energy. I would have to have crawled out of the abyss, my will overcoming all obstacles. I needed a literate energy that I did not possess just then.

Three: I could attempt to comply, become so negligible he needn't fear me. I opted for the third;

"I'll try," I mumbled. "I won't telephone you or visit unexpectedly or do anything that might confuse you,"

but as soon as he was gone I knew it was impossible to be that small, so everything was impossible. On my wedding anniversary I had committed myself to another love failure, a terrible mistake

so I reneged. I opted for the denouement. I dialled his number and a woman answered. At first I thought I had the wrong number but then I remembered my line. She said "Hello" to prompt me. I said, "Hello?"

At first I forgot my next line. Then I remembered, "Is Klaus there?"

Klaus, I knew, was there. It was a rhetorical question. I could have improved on it. I could have asked for Mr. Klaus or Rev. Klaus or I could have used my pet name, asked for the visitor, but humour is not appreciated in the denouement. This was no laughing matter. Sarcasm was out too. The line had to be delivered straight, "Is Klaus there?" There was another pause. She had forgotten her next line now. Then she remembered. "Klaus, it's for you." Of course it was for him; this was his apartment.

Perhaps I should have improvised. "Tell Klaus my grandmother died last night so I'll be away for three days so our dinner date is off. Actually, everything's off. Sorry. Tell him

I'm sorry." I could try to be polite—I always try to be polite—or I could have given her the message "Just tell Klaus my period started. He'll be happy to hear that!" But this improvisation would have led to another scene and this was supposed to be the denouement; there aren't supposed to be subsequent scenes. I left it, "Is Klaus there?"

The next several lines did not matter. It was all form and no content. The content had all gone before. All that was left was the form: "I can't talk now." "No, of course not." "Well, have a good day." "You too."

I still have my work, but damn it, I'd made a deliberate choice never to work the way you do, as an escape from my body, but to begin with what is physically honest and write from my body. So that's another failure. It's autumn and everything that hasn't been harvested dies in the frost.

Love, Lois

*

1 November

Dear Lois,

Lois, it's a shame you weren't raised Catholic; you would understand God no better, but at least you might understand sin. We pay for it with real money and labour. You scorn my attempt to work my way free, but work works. Think as I do and you might at least finish your book. Look at what is happening instead. You're miserable and Frances doesn't have so much as an acceptable outline from you.

As an experiment, put yourself *out there*. Choose words as mere signifiers, just as William's photos merely signify that he was there, and that those people were there, in that condition.

Put down some statistics, grab at a few poignant images and expand. People want a slice of life; there's no need to offer them the whole pie. Even if you bake such a pie, it can't be digested. A taste is enough.

To the end, I'll contend that language is social while experience is private, that there's no hope for the communion to which you aspire. Words of consecration are spoken but communion is taken in silence. Charlotte sits across the room from me now. She's sucking the slices of orange I've cut for her. The light hits half her face, making her nose appear sharp, which is what I find beautiful in her face, but if I were to say just now "Je t'aime, Charlotte," I would transform the situation into a fiction, no matter how sincere the expression. Even if I took your twist, common enough, and tried to turn this love towards God so my own experience would implicate some transcendent reality, all is lost in the attempt. Charlotte gets up to make us coffee. I purchased fresh croissants and she finds them on the counter. Although her back is turned to me I can see she is arranging them on the plate among the orange slices. Helpless with food, she still takes care to create a playful arrangement she'll present to me without a word, setting the plate, which will remain untouched, in easy reach on the coffee table between us. I am speechless.

Finish your book, Lois, and I'll finish my love affair with Charlotte, because soon you must make more money and I will be a father and must return to Toronto.

I fear for you. This visitor of yours has again become conflated with God. Receptivity towards one, in your mind, becomes receptivity towards both, and the reverse seems equally true; when your visitor disappoints you, proving to be the slime I suggested he might be some months ago, you are disappointed in God. This must be some sort of clitoral logic, or perhaps it goes deeper, a meeting of disparate realities that occurs in your womb, and you hope to birth a new order. Why do I even try to understand? I am not physically equipped, and in any case you will do what you will with your visitor, with your book and with your God. Let me just say though, that if my story is a murder mystery, Lois, yours is *Frankenstein*.

    With love, J.P.

*

Dear Jean-Philippe,   November 13

please don't be stupid. When a man refers to a woman's womb I know he's about to be stupid. To speak of a woman's sexual organs in the singular demonstrates as much acceptance as a hick who blushes as he mumbles, "You know, down there." But what is, of course, most off-putting is your dismissive reference to my clitoris, a locus of my desire for my visitor and, maybe you are right, also for God,

something you know nothing about. But there are other organs, lungs for instance, and most acutely the digestive organs, entrails, stomach, etc., that equally confound metaphor and are common to men and women. You take something in as nutrition, but when is it in you and when does it become you? Basically, if our form were simplified we'd be donut-shaped and can consider what passes through our mouth, throat, stomach, intestines and anus as *out there*. The appropriation occurs chemically, molecularly, ultimately subatomically. Ultimately, we have no idea what is out there and what is in here,

just as you had no real idea what was happening when you entered Margaret's vagina and your sperm subsequently entered Margaret's uterus so a part of you was left behind, meeting a part of her, perhaps the next day while you yourself were sitting in a library, and a foetus was conceived partly you and partly Margaret but mostly itself, so this isn't just my problem, J.P.,

and when I take a lover there is the same sort of confusion of space, and I have no language for this. I can't delineate inner and outer space precisely, but we speak as if we do, all our words. We've never taken women as physically normative, have ignored the inherent ambiguity of sexuality, digestion, never mind breathing. And if physical boundaries are fictions, then what is private property or national boundaries and what are the boundaries of consciousness?

answer me that and I'll get straight down to work. I'll be precise as hell about the famine in Eritrea. They're predicting up to five million more deaths. You answer me and I'll explain why we should care.

In the mean time, how can I write a book about famine when I don't understand sex and digestion? How can I write anything, unless I site a particular location in space or different organs in a body that I claim to be mine, as if I accept the convention that there is property in a body, that this is mine, and then with this detachment I can even write from different organs as distinct tones and genres. Now, for instance, in my fury I am all stomach and my words are bilious. But why I am angry with you I cannot say, so it subsides and I begin writing with my lungs; I sigh. You are obviously in love with Charlotte and I am sorry.

I just finished reading a book about world hunger that was organized around myths about hunger, myths meaning lies I suppose, rather than ancient truths. The entire book is a dialectic, what the fictional opposition believes (what the authors believe others believe) in contradiction to what the authors believe. Surprisingly, but perhaps this doesn't surprise you, while the agenda is set by the imagined opposition, the authors make their points and it is quite satisfying to read. Of course the hungry people aren't satisfied. They presumably are still hungry, or dead,

but one can appropriate the authors' ideas. I read that starvation isn't due to a lack of food but to a lack of democracy, economic as well as political democracy, and the idea appeals to me precisely because it is an idea, in the realm of things that can be manipulated (if ideas are things) the way matter never succumbs to facile stratagems for change, but then perhaps change doesn't first occur in matter (clearly nature presents the modern world with small problems to solve if compared to the big problems the modern world presents to nature)

and whatever we think is nearly possible; that is another problem, because our imaginations spin off and we are subject to nightmares. The evil in our lives begins with us as a dream.

J.P., I am too much provoked to write to you now.

Love, Lois

*

23 November

Dear Lois,

Charlotte is writing her papers. You are writing angry letters to me. Everyone is writing except me. Frances explained that I missed the mark with the outline for my murder mystery, my characters lacking authenticity. She even went so far as to suggest I take a teaching job when I come to Toronto, to give the idea a rest.

Don't think I am totally unsympathetic, Lois. I face similar dilemmas in my work and, like you, I find the more I think about them the worse they become. Take this issue of authentic characterizations that Frances raised. Last night a man walked into the bar, a real character. That is what I thought of him and that is what called my attention to the expression, a real character. Perhaps your point about words applies more generally to *things* to which we also attribute meaning, that they create this quality of inauthenticity. The man had long black hair, curly but carefully groomed, bushy black eyebrows, dark skin. He's Latin, I thought, or wants to appear to be Latin, but I could not be sure. He was swaddled in a long black cape with a satin collar and a long black scarf. No kidding. I recognized, as I jotted down this description in my notebook, that the more expressive the attire or the vocabulary, the less reality seems to persist. The man's cape might have been altogether hollow—certainly nothing he said to the bartender suggested otherwise—yet I insist on the expression, he is a real character.

Another case in point: Charlotte was in love with a young man last year. In fact, and it leaves a bad taste in my mouth, this was his apartment which Charlotte decorated to please him. He was tall and attractive, his Parisian accent part of his general appeal, I'm afraid, along with a billfold stuffed with credit cards which enabled Charlotte and him to dine in expensive restaurants instead of in the college cafeteria where her other chums gathered. He explained that he was living on funds from his deceased parents' estate, administered by a lawyer in Paris as long as he was attending business college in Montreal. Once he graduated he would receive the entire inheritance and planned to set up a chain of boutiques specializing in Parisian fashion imports across Canada. According to Charlotte, the situation was explained to her in considerable detail. He studied spreadsheets on his home computer. He received the latest trade and fashion mags from Europe. He set off to classes every day. Eventually the phone was cut off because the bill hadn't been paid. He said Bell had made a mistake. When the landlord threatened to evict them he wrote to his lawyer in Paris demanding an explanation for why the rent hadn't been paid promptly. Then Charlotte discovered, having called the registrar to reach "Ed" in class one day, that he wasn't enrolled. They'd never heard of him. She confronted "Ed" and he called the registrar a liar. The next day, while she was in classes, he moved out. She wrote to his lawyer in Paris, who had pressed a fraud charge against "Ed" there. In court she was one complainant among a half-dozen department stores, credit agencies and Bell. She was heart-broken but months later, even now I suppose, she wonders who broke her heart. She doesn't deny that she was in love, but questions with whom. She is still furious, but at whom?

Charlotte's experience with "Ed" might explain her hostility when I explained the notion you and I share, that we invent ourselves. Yet anyone who reflects upon their conscious process confronts the simple truth that while our inventiveness is situated in time, we seem to be constantly operating outside of time. Einstein merely offered physical proof for what is asserted in an ancient belief of reincarnation: existence is not determined by either our body in a particular state, or by circumstance. We travel faster than the speed of light repeatedly, every day, thereby altering both circumstance and time, moving into the past through the force of memory and into the future through the power of our imaginations.

So let us make our peace, Lois. I was wrong to offer you advice; I admit that. Talking with Frances I recognized the simple truth, that while your thoughts seem in chaos your life is neat as a pin. I, on the other hand, don't know where I'll be living next week, and for the moment Charlotte wants me to proofread her term paper. I will write again soon.

Love, J.P.

*

December 16

Dear Jean-Philippe,

Hold your praise. My favourite poet suggests we shouldn't accept praise while we're still alive, for it is by way of conclusion, and all conclusions during one's life are premature. And as for myself, I'm buffeted in my heart and mind by my errors, a series of philosophical sins, J.P., that I must confess if I'm ever to be capable of writing anything again, let alone if I am to know how to live. Bear with me while I put them into words which are, of course, the source of so many philosophical errors, so much grief. Ambiguity is everywhere, since words can signify what is either honest or not honest and nothing in the signifier seems to signify the difference. Let me offer an example:

an honest statement was made by my visitor, "I went on a holiday." What was also true was that he and his wife went on a holiday, while I had assumed that the speaker was single, since he used the singular pronoun and is indeed a most singular man. The fact that he is married isn't disclosed until months later when nothing that pertains to pronouns really matters any more.

Then there is the knotty issue of metaphor, the richest corruption of logic but inseparable from language, suggesting that this is like that when this is always about as much like that as like any number of other things and remains in fact this rather than that. Take famine:

I might say I made some specific choices because I was starved for affection but I'm not going to die from my hunger and it's appalling to compare my erotic fantasies with the hunger of those who will. Anyway, we could spin off into eternity, and have, discussing my philosophical errors and the resulting chaos in the area of linguistics, but let me move on.

A far more grievous error, and there is none more persistent in my thinking, is idealism. It is almost impossible to refute idealism on its own terms. Everything is as we think it is and not as we think it is not, everything existing as a shadow of what is real in itself when what is really real is our idea of its essential nature. It is such a pretty idea. It produces a relaxing philosophical stasis (not to mention some fine novels that are internally consistent) within me wherein nothing changes so long as I don't change my mind about how things are. I can hang there, not realizing that within the stasis I am stuck. Days pass. Months. Finally the only thing that moves me, the only thing that can knock me out of that coma-like stasis, is body contact. Flesh touching flesh transforms my idealism almost instantaneously, all hell breaks loose, and it is proven to be an error no matter what idea I had. I fall out of error just to fall into yet another error:

solipsism. Solipsism is the sensualist's idealism, the belief that the world exists as a reflection of my own internal reality. It is a philosophical advance in relation to idealism, in that I recognize that the world does exist even if its existence cannot be proven, only felt. But there is almost an infinite number of internal realities, whereas it seems the world cannot abide infinities; it presents us with finitude at every turn. If I do this then I simply cannot do that also, and I can't undo this either. (What I love about the new physics is that it posits the possibility of escaping this dilemma, suggests that I could go back in time to a time when I hadn't done that, if only I could move fast enough, faster than light.) However, the finest quality of solipsism is that it is almost always self-correcting, given time. I can illustrate this point with a recent occurrence that I will name "A Sound Refutation of Solipsism":

I wake up wanting to nibble on my lover's toes and, realizing that it is a clear crisp day, which I understand is an affirmation of my desire, I skip over to his home and find him there, bringing a Christmas tree up onto his porch with the assistance of his lover, who I now realize is also his wife. But I am there now too. I cannot not be there. And the sun does not stop shining. And a freak windstorm doesn't occur, swooshing down, ripping the porch away from the wall, nor does my body defy its own solidity and vaporize as I realize the mistake I have made. And since I can't just disappear I am invited in for tea, to sit down on this nice couple's couch with my cup trembling in my hand as they prop the tree up into its stand in the living-room window, and there is no denying that there are three separate realities—his, hers and mine—but only one living room on this clear wintry day. The error is seen for what it is and

we come to existentialism. This is it, what I've been coming to for years: the firm conviction that we choose our own reality and have no one to blame but ourselves. This is the great and terrible morning-after solipsistic revelry. It is muscular. I buck up, insist I can take it, that I'm strong that way. It is, I realize, the philosophical error of those who are born lucky. Practically no one born into a revolution, war, famine or housing crisis believes in existentialism. Practically no one raising children believes in it for long either. But those who feel themselves in firm control of their own fate cannot resist the allure of existentialism—nor could I, for a time—and this is the considerable overlap between solipsism and existentialism

but I do have children and face a housing crisis, so where does this leave me? It is morning. Another great morning-after. If one has not bought cereal or fresh bread or coffee to perk that could soften the hard edge of existential reality on this morning-after, and if one is so unlucky as to have to get a manuscript to her publisher which is not complete, and to be responsible for her children's breakfast, and must harangue the landlord because there is no hot water, and if it is not a lovely day—in fact, sleet is pounding against a broken pane of glass in the window—then this is when philosophy with all its errors gives way to visions of Kali, the Hindu god who emerges from the Ganges river, quite pregnant, and immediately gives birth, tenderly suckles her infant, then stuffs the baby into her mouth, crushing and swallowing it before she dives back into the river's water, out of sight.

This vision is not a philosophical solution; it has nothing to do with philosophy, but it suggests resolution. One resolves to make a grocery list. One calls the landlord and loses one's temper. One makes french toast, stale bread dipped in eggs, for the children and, as if there is some mercy, the children do not quarrel and are delighted to have french toast for a change, chirping some lovely consolation. Then one dresses, finishes whatever letter is in the typewriter, calls one's publisher and, if one is good at this, can make up a good lie.

Best wishes. Love, Lois

*

22 December

Dear Lois,

    I see. Congratulations. Your love affair continues to disappoint you but at least you now recognize bad love doesn't necessitate a career change.

    I will be coming into Toronto early in the new year before the baby is due. I might take you up on your offer and stay with you temporarily, until I can find a place of my own, but keep an eye out for an apartment. I'll make some calls myself from here.

    In the mean time, finish that damn book, Lois. I can't stand listening to your reasons for not finishing it. Please. When I get to Toronto, if it isn't already finished, we'll sit down together and bang out the few additional pages of text, quote the experts and be done with it. I don't mean to be presumptuous but you have worked too long already to quit. Please, write no more about it; write it. And stop fucking married men. Do those two things and everything will be fine. I'll be seeing you soon. Merry Christmas.

    Love, J.P.

PART II. PAROLE

It's almost midnight, January 7th, when J.P. arrives. He had planned to return to Toronto by February but Margaret suffered toxaemia, was hospitalized New Year's Day, and this morning a slightly premature labour was induced. Stephanie was born at four in the afternoon while J.P. was packing, clearing out of Charlotte's apartment to take the evening train to Toronto.

The medical emergency and the weight of first-time fatherhood buttressed J.P.'s resolve to behave in an exemplary adult manner, or so I gathered from our telephone conversation, when it was decided he would move in with us temporarily. He hesitated, unwilling to impose, until I reminded him that his funds had enabled me to procure the apartment just eight months earlier. He then gratefully accepted my offer.

As for my own children, who are now in their second cycle of deep sleep, I told them that J.P. will be staying with us for an unspecified length of time. This information I couched in terms deemed appropriate for children, which is tantamount to ensuring that they won't feel comfortable enquiring about the nature of our relationship.

I leave the front door unlocked so the children won't be disturbed by the doorbell. Jean-Philippe lets himself in, enters the drafty front hall, is clumsily depositing his bags there as I open the door to our flat to meet him.

—Well, hello ... and uh, congratulations.

—Hi ... Uh ... God, it's cold.

He kisses me on both cheeks, a custom I'm not accustomed to, so my nose mashes awkwardly against his. —Shit. Sorry.... Bring your stuff in here ...

—What ...

—What're you missing?

—I think I left my sack ... No, here. Good.

—The box.

—Yeah, thanks. Uh ... Lois, it's good to see you ... Let me get my stuff outta the way here.

—Just slide it inside the door.

—I've got something. Let me see. In the sack ... here.

—Oh Jean, it's . . .
—A lamp.
—A lamp?
—A lamp.

His gift to me is a bouquet of plastic flowers with a small white light set in each bloom.

—Uh . . . where does the bulb go?
—You don't like it.
—No, it's great. You know I love flowers . . . never tried plugging them in before.
—You're hard to please, Lois.

Now I kiss him on one cheek. —God's sake, come on in. It's cold.

—Uh . . . Here.
—Look, leave this stuff . . . Good . . . Let's . . . the kitchen's back there.

As we pass by the living room J.P. looks in. —Nice door.
—Coffee's on. Thick as tar . . . You want some scotch?
—Please.
—You brought something for the kids, I hope.
—Candy . . .
—Great.
—Uhh . . . and a VCR.
—A VCR?
—Yeah, Charlotte gave it to me.
—Charlotte gave you a VCR?
—Yeah. Her psychopath left it.
—Oh.
—It's probably hot. Everything in her place he'd stolen, one way or another.
—And now you've stolen it from her?
—No. She gave it to me.
—We don't even have a TV.
—You don't?
—It broke.
—Then what'll I do with this?
—I don't know.

—Oh.

—Just put it on the floor over there.

He follows me into the kitchen. —I brought your kids some chocolates.

—Good. They won't let you stay otherwise.

—It's okay with them, me staying?

—If you bring candy.

—Well, I did. They in bed?

—It's past midnight.

—Heh, I got to find . . .

—The washroom?

—No, the chocolate.

I pour the scotch while J.P. sits down at the kitchen table and the chair padding exhales. —Give it to them tomorrow.

—God, I'm tired. What time is it?

I bend down to look at the clock in the microwave and his eyes follow mine, reading the clock for himself, and then our eyes meet. —Maybe you should get to bed. With a new baby . . . better grab sleep when you can.

—No problem. Margaret's on her own with the night stuff.

—Wait and see.

—No. She made that clear.

—Hmm . . .

—Yeah, well, forget it . . . I'm fine . . . Shit, this is really awful . . .

—Give it some time.

—No, I mean this glass. You steal it from Honest Ed's?

—No, Diane made it at camp.

—Oh . . . sorry.

I settle in across the table from him. —So J.P., how are you?

—Depressed.

—Yeah?

—Talked to Margaret on the phone.

—Uh-hmm?

—Well, we're not getting back together.

93

—Maybe Stephanie'll have colic . . .

—Anything wrong with the baby, I blame Schwartz's . . . In those first few months Margaret ate her weight in nitrates, no kidding.

—The baby's fine.

—Well heh, what do we know? This scotch is great.

—Ah . . . To life. (We clink the ice in our glasses, a rueful toast.)

—Yeah . . . You look great, Lois.

—Thanks.

—You fine?

—Sure . . . Fine.

—Umm, good.

I offer J.P. a refill. —Some more?

—So, Lois, how do I look? Tell the truth.

—Uh . . . tired . . . put on a few pounds . . . You look better.

—Like an old man who has been fucking a girl-child . . . Admit it, Lois. I look like hell.

—Fine.

—God . . .

—So how's Charlotte doing?

—She's off to Paris in a few months . . . I could meet her there.

—You going to?

—Eh, I'm a father now . . .

—Not a death sentence.

—No, well . . . (pouring more scotch) I gotta get a job or something.

—Hmm . . .

—A grant or something . . .

—Heh, did I congratulate you yet?

—I haven't got it yet.

—No, I mean on the baby.

—Eh, nothing to it.

—So . . . you and Margaret talked?

—No. Well . . .

—No, eh?

—Well, I called a couple of times since she's been in hospital ... told you that ... Nothing new. She hasn't changed a bit ...

We are sitting back on the kitchen chairs and can hear the clock tick, the furnace switch on. I pour both of us more scotch.

—You know, I don't know if I'd go back anyway. I mean, it was worth talking about, with the baby and all, but ...

I lean back on my chair. —J.P., I'm jealous.

—You want another baby?

—No, I want someone waiting for me in Paris.

His voice deepens and he raises his glass. —Oh no, Lois. We're too old for this.

—Yeah, well ...

—Yeah, *really*.

—Is it true, Jean?

—What?

—Does their skin spring back when you touch it?

—Hah, it's all true; doesn't make a dent ... They can do it all night still. God, it's all true. I'm so tired.

—Me too. I was going to work tonight, but I think I'll crash. You want a shower?

—In the morning.

—The back room's set up for you. My computer's in my room, in the front. Hell, you need a proper tour.

—Tomorrow.

—Anyway, I left you the desk. And you've got your own entrance back there. Heh, look back here anyway. (We get up. The door to his room is already ajar.) There.

—Looks great.

I move towards the front hall. —There's towels and sheets on the bed. The bathroom's just down those stairs.

—Shit, thanks.

—No problem.

He puts his arm around my shoulder. —You're too good to me.

—Would you stop?

—It's true. You're ... He picks up his suitcase and

yawns. —Anyway, while I'm here maybe you could go to Ethiopia. Maybe a trip would put you over the top with that book.

—Don't be ridiculous.

—No? Well anyway, I'm crashing. Heh, where do you want me to put these?

J.P. picks up his electric bouquet with a grin, so before we retire we have to set it up beside the couch in the living room. J.P. complains again that I don't have a television, and puts the VCR box in a likely spot for a set. While he's fixing the bulbs in the lamp I go back and get our glasses and the bottle. We pour ourselves one last drink, put on a tape and listen to Errol Garner's piano in the incandescent glow of J.P.'s blossoms.

*

The next morning I wake up to Diane's clarinet. I'm disoriented, having left my alarm clock in J.P.'s room. The smell of coffee and pancakes wafts through the living room as I move towards the kitchen and look in from the doorway. J.P.'s at the stove and Diane, who greatly admires him, is perched on a stool playing a bit of Bartók for him. Daniel's sitting at the table with chocolate smeared on his face, candy wrappers and a plate of rolled crêpes in front of him and his fingers stuck in his ears. He sees me first.

—Make her stop, Mom.

—You say what, Duffus?

—Eh, look who's up.

—Morning.

—Here, Lois. Coffee's ready.

—Diane, a bit early for music.

—J.P. likes it, and Murphy's hearing solos today. Gotta practise.

—Here's another for you, princess. Eat up. What time you kids have to be out of here?

—Eight-fifteen.

—Not me. I don't gotta go till ten to nine. I'm meeting Josh.

J.P. glances at the clock on the microwave, and then looks back at Diane. —Hmm.... Hey, you're getting syrup in your mouthpiece there.

—Oops.

—Daniel, you not hungry?

—Can't eat with my fingers in my ears.

I sit down. —Eat, Daniel. You'll be late.

J.P. sets a steaming mug in front of me. —Here's coffee, crabby lady.

—They're tiny. They're toony ...

—Oh God, Mom, don't let him start singing that stupid song again.

—Mom, J.P.'s got a VCR and he's getting us a television.

—He is, is he?

—So I can watch Tiny 'Toons!

—I'm off, Mom. Thanks, J.P. You be here tonight?

J.P. holds Diane's sack up as she slips her arm through the strap. —Sure.

—Great. Love you, Mom.

Diane pecks my cheek, and Daniel wipes his mouth on his arm, grabbing his jacket. They're off. It's Monday. Jean-Philippe sits down.

—God, that's weird. It's totally noisy, and then it's totally quiet.

—Normal.

—Weird.

—More coffee there?

—I think so.

—What're you up to this morning?

—Called the hospital. Margaret's still asleep but I got the room number.

He puts a scrap of paper on the table between us.

—Everything fine?

—Guess so. Stephanie's going to be rooming in sometime today so they shortened visiting hours.

—Not for the fathers.
—Yeah? Well, they didn't know ... They do now. I didn't know the room number or anything ... Hell, it's the 1990s, right?
—Uh-huh.

*

—You want to come down with me? See the baby? (I look up, brow furrowed) ... No ... well, you've got work to do ... Another time... So, I'm a coward. Excited as hell. I'm meeting my daughter today! Do I look like hell? Don't want her thinking I'm a mess.
—She won't notice.
—Margaret will.
—Yeah, well, better shave.
—Shit, yeah ... You need the bathroom?
—No. Go ahead.
—Yeah ... well ... Great, eh?

*

The flat that we inhabit consists of the first floor and finished basement of a large Victorian home in Parkdale. It is surprisingly spacious; everyone has their own room and access to the bathroom, kitchen and outdoors. My room, the front room on the first floor, is now divided to provide a discreet working area and a sleeping area, with a separate doorway into the front hall, so I can enter or leave without passing through the rest of the flat. I have given over my office in the back, behind the kitchen, to Jean-Philippe who has access to the outdoors through the backyard and alley. Diane's and Daniel's bedrooms, the bathroom and a hall lined with bookshelves and fish tanks are in the basement.

In the beginning virtually all our communal life transpires in the kitchen, situated between the living room and back room. It is painted light grey with dusty peach trim. The formica counters were not replaced when the kitchen was updated; they remain a garish red with black marbling, cracked in two places. The kitchen window looks onto the neighbour's kitchen but is covered with white lace sheers to provide both households a modicum of privacy. There are herbs growing poorly by the window, since there is insufficient light. The rest of the room, one might say, is pert. Several years ago a potter friend made me a set of dishes, having his assistant lay her body down on a large slab of clay which he moulded around her extremities. The slab was cut up into four irregular-shaped place settings that rest on an open shelf above the kitchen sink. Glasses and mugs rest on the narrow shelf beneath that, and vases and various antique pieces clutter the highest shelves. Books darkened by kitchen grease stand on bookshelves along the far wall and an assortment of wind-up toys, for which my children and I have developed a fondness, are interspersed among the volumes. Nothing visible except the appliances is of any obvious utility. Cooking pots are stashed beneath the oven.

On the third afternoon after Jean-Philippe's arrival, I come into the kitchen and find him pouring Diane and himself a glass of milk.

—Mom, look at these pictures.
—Daniel downstairs?
—Hi.
—I've got to . . .
—J.P.'s baby.
—Yeah?
—Cute, eh? Except her eyes are funny.
—You think . . .
—Heh, you said so. It's the drops.
—Let me see . . . Hey, look at that.
—What you think?
—She's beautiful, Jean.

He's grinning. I pat him on the back.

—Daniel better . . . Heh, Danny!

J.P. holds a baby picture up next to his ear and grins, but Diane is looking at another photo on the table. —She's something, eh? . . . Here, Diane . . . . Look at this one . . . You see any resemblance?

—That your wife, J.P?

—Yeah.

—God, she looks awful.

—Yeah, well . . .

—What's she doing? . . .

—Diane!

J.P. puts the picture back down on the table and crosses over to the refrigerator, opening the door. —Lois, you want some milk? Some coffee?

—Got to do something first.

—Boy, you must be happy . . .

—Daniel, save some water for the fish!

—Mom, he can't hear you down there . . . You got to really scream . . . Daniel, get the hell out! Mom's got to go!

Muffled sounds emanate from Daniel in the bath downstairs.

—What?

—J.P., can I have a biscuit?

—Sure. They're in that box there.

—You must be so excited.

Diane opens the box and begins noshing on a cookie. —You going to move in with them?

—Diane, mind your own business.

—I don't know, love. I'd like to . . .

—Diane, don't you have to practise? Go on now.

—Sorry, J.P. Mom only reminds me to practise if I'm being rude.

—Move it.

—Heh, you want to come to my next concert? I'm selling tickets. Just five bucks . . .

—Diane, what happened to the tickets I already paid for?

Jean, I've got six. You can have one of mine.

—Oh, yeah. I forgot.... Great baby pictures, J.P. You going to bring the baby here? I'll babysit... Oh, sorry Mom, that's none of my business either, I guess. See you... I'm at Mannie's, Mom. Bye.

Diane leaves with her clarinet case. A whirl of noise follows her out the door. I continue pacing between the top of the stairs, to see when Daniel's out of the washroom, and the kitchen. J.P. is looking over the baby pictures.

—You must be proud.

—Here. Let me clear a spot.

—Don't worry... She really is cute.

—You going to visit?

—Well, how much longer are they in hospital?

—I don't know. Margaret's not sure. They say... What a mess....

—This is weird.

—She even bit her lip and it was bleeding... She's got stitches in her side and her bottom. Explain that, will you?

—Hmm...

—Well, I'm not going to ask... Anyway, they say they're both fine.

—You okay?

—Yeah, well... sure.

I walk to the top of the stairs to shout down to Daniel in the washroom. —Just a second, J.P. Daniel!... Never mind; he can't hear me.

When I move back to the table and sit down across from him, J.P. stares up at me. —She's offensively polite. I mean... Well... What else can we do?

—All things considered, you are doing pretty well.

—She assumes I want visiting rights. Saturdays... I said fine.

—Sounds good.

—Pass me some of those biscuits, will you?

—Sure.

—I've never felt so... Stephanie's back in the nursery

but I looked in on Margaret. She's got this pain... With me it's all polite; the nurse explained, and I could see she was pissed off... this nurse, a waspy little bitch... I suppose she thinks it's all my fault.

—Maybe you're sensitive now.

—No. Her stiff white face under a stiff white hat, speaking with sharp consonant endings. Christ...

—She wears a nurse cap? That says something...

—Yeah? I think Daniel's done down there.

—It's okay.

—Well, I felt absolutely rotten... Look, I'm not gonna let it get to me.

—Good.

—I mean, I can't get over my daughter. Look at this... He picks up another photo.

—Who took the snaps?

—They've got someone who goes around. Oh, I took that.

—She's something...

—Yeah, this is *my* baby... that's weird.

—Yeah. It's great.

—Yeah? Don't take this wrong. I mean, I know she's mine, but it's so cognitive. Look here, look at Margaret.

—Don't mind Diane...

—I know. But look. She's wiped and there's no doubt what's happening. She was even awake for the caesarean... and now this pain... but for her it doesn't matter at all. It just *is*.

—Is that what Margaret said about it?

—No. She's polite as hell. Like it's nothing, and for me I guess it *is* nothing since it's her pain, not mine, which is exactly the way she wants it, like it's got nothing to do with me...

—Well...

He takes another biscuit. —So there's nothing to it.

—Hmm...

—I left that nurse straightening the sheets so Margaret could start twisting and winding them up again, like it's a shroud.

—Hmm . . .

—They're a pain team, those two . . .

—You want me to call? Ask what's happening?

—No. If Margaret wanted us to know she'd say. Anyway, Stephanie's fine. Look, I bought us some champagne. About time we celebrated. What do you say? . . . You want some to go with these biscuits? Try one. They're delicious. I got them for Margaret but she said she wouldn't eat them . . . and they don't allow alcohol.

—Daniel, you done down there?

*

One late afternoon the kids and I are lolling on the floor in the living room when J.P. arrives, concealed behind and beneath a large cardboard box. We can't see anything but his legs as he enters, and he bumps his arm against the right edge of the doorjamb, then again on the left edge. The box is labelled JVC and, given its size, it obviously contains the promised television. While we relieve J.P. of his burden and tear at the staples on the lid, Diane seems impressed with J.P.'s generosity, Daniel is ecstatic, and I worry about noise levels.

—Where should I put it?

—God, this is great, J.P. Thanks.

—Not there. Look, it's right outside my door.

—Over here?

—I'll still hear it.

—Ah, Mom. You love 'em.

—Not in the morning.

—Who?

—Spielberg.

—Tiny 'Toons!

—Spielberg.

—What time's it on?

—Seven-thirty.

—Night?
—A.m.
—Saturday?
—Every day.
—You're kidding?
—I think the set should go straight into J.P.'s room, kids. He'll watch it with you.
—Great idea!
—How about the living room?

*

For the next few weeks we move between the kitchen and the living room. News of the pending Persian Gulf war frequently interrupts the scheduled shows. It is understood that to complain is unpatriotic; our contribution to the war effort will be to watch.

A week passes. J.P. is making the two of us omelette for lunch and I am reading at the kitchen table. The microwave beeps notice that the potatoes are cooked. I startle and J.P. takes the opportunity to grab my attention.

—I still don't get it.
—What?
—You know ... how you do it ... I mean, I don't feel like I know ... Who pays the groceries around here?
—Lately? You do.
—Amazing.
—A miracle.
—When's Michael coming back?
I look up. —To Toronto, you mean?
—Yeah.
I stick my face back in my book. —Or to me?
—Does he send money?
—Some. It's fine ...
—Really?
—Really. Eventually I'll sell the lot up north and then I'm set.

—It seems somehow insubstantial...

—Well, it's not your concern, really.

—I know. It's just... I don't know...

I close my book and put it down on the table. —Look, J.P....

—Sorry.

—You always worry about that stuff... You want me to worry?

—No. I mean, that's your lawyer's job.

—I quit the lawyer.

—How...

—It's fine.

—Sure... Well, sure... It's just...

—Look, I do make money. That's why I was reading this book.

—Oh, yeah, sorry.

—Okay.

He puts two plates on the table, one in front of me and the other at the end of the table so he can sit close to the stove. There's a second omelette frying. —Well... so how's everything in Eritrea?... Food's on.

—The situation's changing, I guess. Always is. The one thing that's always the same. Gorbechev was a wild card. Now maybe a war.

—Hmm, yeah. Heh, eat up before it gets cold.

I put a forkful of omelette in my mouth. —I am. Hmm, this is good...

—Hmm. Yeah.

—You ever notice, J.P., how constant change comes to look like stasis?

—Yeah.

—And it's funny but stasis, when nothing's really happening, seems to move like a ballet or something, really graceful like that, when there's nothing changing.

—Salt?

—Yes, please... Take the newspaper. If I read it every day it's full of news; things are happening. But I leave it for a few weeks and then pick it up some day, and everything's the same. Weeks have passed. There's a pile of papers, all news, new things that have happened, but nothing has changed; nothing really happens.

—Yeah. I don't read it every day.

—Or leave off with some friend for a while, when nothing's happening, and then you find out all sorts of things have changed.

—Maybe that's what you see in William's Eritrean photos.

—You can't see it. We don't have senses for it ... but still, maybe a sense of it. No, you're right.

—Hmm.

—You sure as hell can't photograph it.

—No?

—Truths move.

—Hmm ...

—Good omelette.

—Thanks. More?

—No. I'm full.

—You just had a bite.

—It was good.

—Does William know you hate his work?

—No.

—It must hurt; I mean, he must sense you dislike it.

—I don't think so. The man's thick ... Deeply shallow.

—I still think you might try his approach. The journalist's.

—Sure, easy. Get the right angle.

—Exactly. Pepper? ... I told you, I'd stay with the kids.

—Why?

—So you could go there.

—Eritrea?

—Sure.

—Why would I?

—To finish the book and get paid.

—Germaine Greer did that, to witness the resettlement. You know what she saw? What no one else saw, or what everyone else saw differently.

—So?

—I love Greer. I love her writing. But do I believe her?

—Well?

—No. There's something wrong with her trip notes. I don't want to do what she did.

—You're not eating... You know, when you get nervous you blink more often.

I take a bite of potato. —Yeah?

—I read that in one of those books... Photos of gestures, can you beat that?

—But I didn't know that, about blinking.

—Yes you did.

—No I didn't.

—You still seeing that married man? See there, you did it.

—Are you trying to pick a fight?

—You're getting another cold sore. There, you blinked twice.

—Can we talk about something else.

—Making you nervous?

—No.

He shakes his fork at me, grinning. —Sure. You're blinking. Look in a mirror.

—Are you sure you have that right?

—Yeah, and you know it. I mean, your eyes know. Still, someone got paid to write a book about that... See, there they go again. You blinked!

—That's stupid.

—But it's true. Every eye knows it, and some guy just writes it down ... like it's news.

—Knowing is more than a reflex.

He stuffs his mouth full, chews. —You know, I'd hate to be you. Anyway, your book's going to be outdated by summer. I read it in the paper; there's a new famine ... twice as many people are going to die as in '84. You read that?

—Yes. It's been looming for a year.

—Will William be going back?

—Why would he?
—To take pictures of the next three million.
—How can you say that with your mouth full?
He swallows. —Maybe you should go with him.
—Why?
—I told you, I'd stay with the kids. We'd get the money together somehow.

I put down my fork as J.P gets up and puts the entire second omelette onto his plate, seeing that I've barely touched my half. —That's beside the point. I've seen people starve . . . I just don't have much to say about it.

—You could write about it. There's grants for that sort of trip.

—That doesn't matter. Besides, it's a waste.

—Look, we're sending all these soldiers the same distance. Surely we can spring for one writer. Go to the war and make a side trip to starvation.

I point to the book next to my plate of eggs. —You know what I read here? Last famine, one of these photographers crouched over a woman for three hours so he could snap his photo the very second she died . . .

*

—Daniel, run tell Diane to get out of there. She's not the only one living here.

—Ah, Mom . . .

Daniel's looking over J.P.'s shoulder at the list he's drawing up.

—Never mind. I'm going down anyway . . . Diane!

She doesn't hear me pounding on the door, and with the water on I can barely hear the conversation at the top of the stairs, but I strain to listen:

—I need to go get a shitload of diapers. Daniel, you want to come with me? My baby's going home tomorrow. Look at this list. I'm going to stock up Margaret's place.

—You need a diaper service. It's better for the environment.

—How do you know?

—TV... A baby's grown up and dead before its plastic diapers decompose.

—Really?

—Yep.

—You know the name of a diaper service?

—Gosh, J.P., I'm only ten.

*

I come into the kitchen and Jean-Philippe is sitting with a plate of muffins and his coffee, reading the *Globe and Mail*. He doesn't look up from his paper, but asks:

—I thought he was married?

I pick up a mug and move over towards the coffee pot but find it's empty. —Who are we talking about?

He closes his paper. —Your friend. You went out last night, and I figured you'd be home early, since he'd have to get home himself... Not that it's any of my business, but I'm an expert on these logistics, you know... and you didn't get in until morning.

—He doesn't live with her, but why do you ask? And how do we know we're talking about the same person?

—A guess.

—The kids get off okay?

—Yep. They do that on their own, do they?

—Yeah. I neglect them.

—You got a zit on your chin. Doesn't this guy ever wash? Okay, you don't want to talk.

—No.

—Okay. You want some breakfast?

—No.

—Coffee?

—I'll make some.

—You got another cold sore, there. This guy really upsets you.

—Are you sure this man we're talking about exists?

—Am I upsetting you? You know, maybe I shouldn't be staying here. I can move soon . . .

—Maybe you can just stop talking to me in the morning.

—It hurts when you talk, with the fever blister and all . . . Sorry . . . I'll make you some eggs.

—I don't want any eggs. Just coffee, thanks. I got to get back to work.

He gets up and takes the pot from me, fills it with water and fills the filter basket with fresh grounds while I sit down with the paper. —Why do you see this guy if it's so upsetting?

—J.P., you said you'd get me coffee.

He switches on the coffee maker. —It'll be just a minute here. You know, Lois, maybe you're not really a lover; you're an explorer.

—J.P . . .

—Oh shit, sorry. I can see you're upset. It's just that living here, I guess it's like . . .

—Don't worry . . .

—I don't know what I can and can't say.

—Form follows function.

—Not really. It confounds function. Actually, form eludes function, wouldn't you say? . . . or maybe over time one erodes the other.

—I suppose that's what's meant by decadence.

—Yeah? Well then, its meaning isn't 'to decay', but 'to despair'.

—Coffee. Jean?

—It takes a minute.

*

—Okay Diane, you wind up the duck and Daniel's got Mickey

Mouse. I've got the rabbit. Okay?

—Ready, Mom.

—Okay. When I say go.... Go!

—He's going to... nope, he turned back. Mom, Mickey's going to kiss the rabbit.

—My duck's heading for the edge.

—Whoever wins chooses the restaurant.

—Mickey kissed the bunny! I win. Pizza!

*

—I would have made dinner.

—We wanted to go out. Besides, you had the baby all day. You must be tired.

—I took her to the library.

—How'd she like it?

—Well, I don't know, but Margaret liked it a lot. She's so tired, it gave her a chance to nap.

—You can bring her here any time, you know.

—Stephanie?

—Yeah, Stephanie. Or Margaret.

—Yeah? We need to talk about that.

—Stay as long as you want. Now have we talked enough?

—I don't know what else to do. I'll get a job and get out, but right now ... I want to spend time with Stephanie while Margaret's not well. But, hey ... you know, I want to pay my share here.

—Fine.

—Sometimes Margaret almost throws Stephanie at me, she's so tired.

—There's plenty of room. Bring her around and Diane will help you watch her. She's crazy about babies.

—What's the matter with your lip?

—I'm getting another cold sore.

—Stress? This is too much, me being here.

—No. Look, I have to get back to work.

J.P. is fingering some photos he took of his daughter on his last visit. —Okay. You work.

—Jean, Stephanie's beautiful.

—She is. She's really beautiful.

*

Margaret recovers very slowly. I don't care to publicize the details, since I maintain a commitment, given the falling birth rate, to minimizing the attention paid to the more difficult areas of child-bearing and child-rearing in Western society. But during these weeks J.P.'s role expands considerably and Stephanie is here several afternoons, some evenings, and when Margaret has to re-enter hospital for a few days Stephanie remains with us. One area of parenting ability in the extreme, I would say, is Margaret's skill in expressing mother's milk, a verb phrase that has always intrigued me. Jean-Philippe is loath to throw out the old milk or to refuse fresh milk so our freezer fills with frozen bottles of the pale blue liquid until eventually I threaten to make custard with the excess.

My children appreciate J.P.'s cooking and his presence, and they enjoy Stephanie, walking her, playing with her, encouraging the few-week-old infant to speak. I am preoccupied with my work during this time. I never see J.P. working. Nevertheless, he manages to complete his manuscript several months before I complete mine, but that is a subject for another essay.

—You know, Lois, when I pick up Stephanie I feel something primitive inside. You hear those stories about men cutting the umbilical cord, biting through it with their teeth. It's like that, and it leaves a bad taste in my mouth.

*

—Mom, come see. A war started.

—Oh, God. They're doing it.

—What?

—See that. You hear that? That's people dying.

—Where?

—Baghdad I guess.

—But...

—There's people living there.

—Where's there?

—See. Diane, pass me the paper there, on the floor... next to... Thanks. See?

—That's Iraq?

—Yeah, and that's Kuwait. See, Iraq went into... there. And now the U.S. says they have to get out, so they're bombing Baghdad.

—There?

—Yeah. Shh....

We're looking back and forth between the newspaper spread between us and the TV. There is very little information on the television news report. After twenty minutes Diane observes, —It sounds like they're enjoying this.

—Yeah, it does.

—I don't get it. It's like there's a fight in the schoolyard and a teacher shows up with a handgun to settle it.

—Daniel, that's pretty much it. But the problem... it supposes the Arabs are kids and the U.S. is adult... more mature.

—Mom, showing up with a handgun means you're mature?

Diane is flicking between stations with the converter. —It's on every station.

—Mom, can we turn this off?

*

After the first night of war, we all agree to a media fast. By providing an audience, we're afraid that we may be encouraging the armies.

J.P. has the children on a steady diet of video movies. The three are watching movies whenever I go out; when I come home they are still staring at the set. Sometimes the children are asleep in front of the TV. J.P. says it won't last, they'll soon run out of movies, but they don't hesitate to watch the same movie over and over. Daniel has seen *Dream a Little Dream* thirteen times. Now J.P. leaves them alone watching movies, and they quarrel about which movie to watch, or what show, so sometimes they are watching one show and taping a TV movie to watch later. I object loudly, first to Jean:

—You see that? I feel like I hardly exist in my own home.
—But you do.
—Exactly.
—I mean . . .
—I mean I can't seem to extricate myself from the logic of this idea here. Your plan, Jean-Philippe, is becoming clear.
—What plan? What logic?
—It all just happens, as in a dream.
—A dream? You call this a dream?
—Wait a minute . . . I read about this in a science book . . . an unsolvable problem, but repeating, something about strange attractors . . . never mind.
—Never mind? I don't mind. You were the one complaining, I just wanted to make us a nice souflée. Wait a minute. . . . Okay. . . . Kids, turn that down.

I follow him into the kitchen. —No. You imagine it is just as you imagined it would be . . . and see? Whatever you cook up, you expect me to eat.
—Lunch? You're talking about supper? I thought you were speaking more generally.
—You don't get it.
—No? Well, you've got to eat.
—Do you ever notice how little of your food I eat?
—But you say it's good.
—But I'm never hungry.

—Well, your kids love it.
—I know that, damn it.
—So eat. Here. It's done.
—Jean, I can't.
—What do you mean, you can't?
—I'm not hungry, that's all.
—Have you had breakfast? Lunch?
—Look, I'm too afraid ... if I start, even if I imagine I start ... Look, for Margaret you said eating was an act of aggression? Well, for me not eating is my line of defence.
—You eat at Klaus's.
—Sometimes.
—So what does he offer?
—Better light. At least there I know what I'm eating.

*

Then, in the end, I set limits on how many hours the children can watch TV: no weekday mornings; two hours at night if their homework is finished; as late as they want on Friday and Saturday. Daniel and I miss watching 'Tiny Toons, but a rule is a rule. Jean-Philippe wants to prove me wrong about television. He brings home educational movies from the National Film Board, the first being a series on Eritrea.
—See the difference?
—You think this is more real?
—Than what?
—Than William's photos.
—No. It's just a different genre. Film and stills. Mainstream photo-journalism ... Revolution.
—Look. The film's made by Canadians ...
—You sure?
—No ... Let's rewind ...
—No. Never mind.
—Diane. What do you think about that?
—The doctor?

—I think she's a nurse.
—It's neat the guys with no legs got something to do.
—Cute baby.

*

One afternoon I walk into the kitchen and sit down next to Daniel who's drinking a glass of milk and eating brownies. I spread out a few of the photos that I've been studying on the table. J.P. is at the sink, moves towards the table and looks over my shoulder at the photo spread.
—Are these William's?
—Yeah. I was supposed to make some suggestions here, for the war section. You like them?
—These two images are . . . the contrast here works better, I think. I don't know . . . What the hell am I talking about?
—Who cares?
Daniel shoves a brownie in his mouth. —Mom keeps looking over them again and again. I think they're gross.
—Fine, Daniel, but don't get your sticky hands . . .
—J.P. Look at this soldier. Mom says he's a teacher.
I put the pictures back in their envelope. —They go back to William tomorrow.
—Lois, you pick up the eggs?
—In the fridge.
—Mom, J.P.'s making spinach souffleé.
J.P. sets the strainer of spinach on the table. —Daniel, you know you're the only kid who likes my spinach souffleé.
—Don't eat that spinach until it's washed.
—It's washed. Hey, Danny boy, run check on Stephanie for me, will you?
—She's not crying.
—That's why I want you to check on her.
—Okay.
—Thanks. . . .
Daniel heads to the living room, where the cot is set up.

116

Once Daniel has left the room J.P. informs me that I've received some mail. —Uh, Lois, there's a letter from Michael under those papers there.

—Oh, thanks.

—He's coming back soon?

—Hmm, let me just read this... Yes... Well, it sounds like he's not sure about travelling, now... well, he wrote this before the war... everything cleared...

—What?

—Oh, things. Legal things... the separation agreement.

—I thought you said you quit that stuff.

—I did but Michael didn't.

—Was it awful?

—What?

—Seeing the lawyer... all that?

—I cried, if that's what you mean by awful.

—When?

—When I signed the papers.

—In your lawyer's office.

—No, on the corner. Bay and Wellesley.

—Why?

—That's where his office is. He does a lot of work for the government.

—But why did you cry?

—I don't know... No one cries there. Everyone rushing around with dry papers for an innocuous government. Everything wet happens somewhere else... Even my tears were dry as documents.

—We're terrible at this, you and I.

—We don't give it our best.

Daniel comes back into the kitchen. —Stephanie's asleep... Hey, where'd you put my brownie?

—Sorry, I thought you were done. It's in the fridge. Get one for your mom while you're at it, will you?

—Hey, Mom, what's up?

—No thanks, hun. I'm not hungry.

    —Eat, Lois. Eat up.
    —I said I'm not hungry.
    —Your mother's upset, Danny.
    —I'm not.
    —Go check on Stephanie.
    —I just did that. She's asleep. Hey, Mom... You okay?
    Daniel touches my back, concerned, so I try to reassure him. —I'm fine, love. Go play.
    —I'll go check on Stephanie again.
    J.P. sits down across from me at the table. —Look, Lois. Finish that book. I'll help you. We can help each other. You scratch my back and I'll scratch yours.
    —Yeah? Well, that's not what itches.

*

—Isn't she lovely when she's sleeping, the little tyrant?
    —I can't believe we finally got her to sleep.
    —What do you mean "we", Lois? I walked her; Diane walked her; Daniel walked her; you went out. I thought babies slept all the time.
    —They used to, but they've changed... Heh, let's not wake her up, thinking she's so beautiful.

*

—Morning, Lois.
    —Morning... the kids got off okay?
    —I guess so. I wasn't up.
    —Christ, I overslept. Almost noon?
    —Diane left you a note from her teacher here.
    —Yeah? God, I worked late...
    —Yeah?
    —Coffee?
    —There's some in the pot there. You were working? I

thought you went out.

I shuffle across the kitchen. —It's not hot. I'll make a new pot.

—There's fresh ground coffee in the freezer.

—Don't get up. Christ... this it? What is this?

—Irish Mocha.

—I hate that kind. It tastes like chemicals.

—I like it.

—I have to go shopping. Make a list and I'll go this morning... Uh, this afternoon.

—Okay.

—What were you doing there?

J.P. looks up at me from his blank notepad. —You say coffee?

—Uh.... What?

—What you want me to write. The list.

— Oh, I don't know...   I was just thinking...

—You know, you never answered my question last night.

—Hmm.... I don't remember. What was it?

—Never mind.

I sit down and take the list away from him. —Well, you didn't answer my question either.

—Which one...?

—About Montreal.

—Shit, I told you, or I wrote to you about it, didn't I?

—No.

—About my sister and my mother? Yes I did.

—Well, if you did it still doesn't make sense to me.

—Actually, I can't talk to mom either, but not because of the French... Never mind. Look, I'll make fresh coffee... I wish we had some real cream.

—I'll put it on the list here...

—You know, Lois, you should go to talk school. Timing is everything.

—We don't have to talk about it.

—Good.

—But you always say you want to talk.

He sets a mug of coffee in front of me and starts rummaging through the cupboards. —Not when you're a zombie. We better get more pablum too.

I write it down and sip the coffee. —It's on the list.

—Don't ever tell Margaret how, with the freezer full of milk, we give Stephanie pablum.

—If you don't want to talk about it we won't.

—Okay. What was the question?

—Why did you make Margaret move?

—I love Montreal. And I didn't think Margaret would turn lunatic on me, eat herself into a stupor and then shove me out. That wasn't the plan.

—Well, she was pregnant.

—Later. She started putting on weight right away.

—I think she got pregnant pretty close to right away.

—No.

—Well, look at the calendar. Look at Stephanie.

The coffee is dripping when he pours himself a cup, so it spills on the burner, sizzling when he sits down across from me at the table. —No. You're wrong. The weight wasn't baby, not in the beginning. It was an act of aggression. She made herself a dragon woman.

—Goethe's eternity.

—What?

—His symbol of eternity. The snake eating its tail.

—What?

—You use it all the time. You insist on it.

—What does this have to do with Goethe?

—His colour theory. He used that symbol . . . I don't know. It was your dream.

—I thought I made it up.

—You're kidding.

—No. Goethe?

—Sure. And long before him, the ouroboros.

—Hmm . . .

—Anyway, when I saw Margaret last summer, if I hadn't

heard so much from you about this weight problem, I would have known she was pregnant, the fact that she wasn't fat; she was pregnant.

—You would have known?

—I think I would have, but I didn't because of everything you said.

—God, Lois, that's spooky.

—Yes, it is.

—Christ, maybe we shouldn't live together if we have this effect on each other.

—Well, you wrote it.

—Not that.

—Yes you did, and then it unfolds and you act like it's an accident.

—You accusing me of something?

—No, unless I'm accusing everybody.

—What?

—It's all so homocentric. We start with an idea, we make it happen, and then we're shocked.

—You catch the news this morning?

—No. The war?

—Yeah. Just wondering . . .

—Let me know when it's over.

—That's lame.

—I won't participate in the show.

—Lois, it's real you know.

—Sure. It scares the hell out of me, and you actually wished it.

—Me?

—You imagined it . . . you've got a powerful imagination.

—You saying I caused the Gulf war?

—Now I know what people mean by that.

—Look, Lois, you're being crazy.

—I'm so tired.

—It's the book.

—I've got to dump it.

—Just finish it. But don't forget, we're two ordinary people here, trying to bring up three ordinary kids, right?

—Right.

—And I didn't start a war.

—But what you imagine . . . it happens . . . Maybe not with everything, but it's frightening to the extent to which it's true.

—Are we now talking about Margaret or the war?

—Actually, I'm thinking about famine, I guess . . . I mean, famine is definitely that. I mean, we, meaning people, do this thing . . .

—Yeah?

—I mean . . . God, we were a bad bet, don't you think? I mean . . . maybe there's also a rabbit Christ, and a turnip Christ, and a star Christ somewhere. Maybe God didn't put all the eggs in this one basket, I mean—the human ovary.

—Does this somehow relate to why I moved to Montreal?

—Instead of staying here and raising a family and tending a garden? I don't know. I'm asking.

—I don't understand the question.

—We make choices and go wild, until it seems like we have no choice about anything, like it's all fated.

—No one accuses you, Lois. You just let things go and does that work so much better?

—You mean Michael?

—Maybe.

—No. You're wrong there, but never mind.

—More coffee?

—You're wrong. We're more alike than you imagine; we just choose the opposite resolution to form.

—You've lost me.

—Well, look at these photos. I mean, there is something really out there and I can't choose what is inside the frame and outside or what to say about that. Absolute beauty and love requires silence . . . and so does evil. So I'm content to stop writing. We don't have the vocabulary . . .

—Better not mention that to Frances....

—It's only one chapter... and there's still desire. I can write about that, but I don't have words for what it is we desire... I know it starts in the body, like hunger.

—Good start.

—Not with freedom or military objectives or our country right or wrong... those things, they're all a matter of choices and that's all we talk about—all we *can* talk about.

—Why don't you just finish the rest of the book and then get back to this chapter.

—Listen, if I were to write about this kind of desire, at the very beginning I would need a new vocabulary, a different syntax...

—You're afraid to just do it.

—Shit, J.P. I can't just do it... and...

—We can't talk about it.

—No, I guess not. It's much worse when we talk. We're so unreflective... the way we omit the subject as if it's understood. It's hardly ever understood.

—You know, Lois, I've been crazy for you to talk to me, but right now...

—Okay. I'm sorry.

—No, just let me get some more coffee...

—Sure.

—Okay... You want some more? Here.... Okay.

—Thanks.

—You know what I think? I think you were sitting up for hours last night... I thought you were out, but no; you were sitting there thinking and thinking until you couldn't write a thing...

—A think...

—Okay. And now you have a point but that's not the point. I suggest you just sit down in front of your computer and do your work and it will come. Whatever the hell it is, it will come... God, see what you do?

—What?

—You get so quiet.

123

—Oh . . .
—Lois?
—It's nothing personal, J.P.
—No? Lois, that is weird. Have you always been like this?
—Isn't everyone?

*

As if to illustrate the point I was trying to make, a few weeks later we have a mid-winter thaw and an exceptionally warm Saturday. Daniel gets out on his bike and Diane is walking Stephanie in the stroller. I am making mushroom soup and J.P. is in his room working. Once Michael returns to Canada, within a month, between four adults there are three children. I am considering the situation as I slice mushrooms. A friend's quip comes to mind: it used to be that parents had a lot of children; now children have a lot of parents. Three children of ill-considered love—with that thought crossing my mind the knife crosses my finger, slicing my finger instead of the mushroom. I cut my finger to the bone. A mushroom doesn't have bone; it doesn't resist a knife or a thought the way I do, but I will not be distracted. I take no notice of the blood dripping on the counter. Remember the thought, I insist, although clearly this is an ill-considered moment to consider ill-considered love. When I notice that the blood is pooling and discolouring the mushrooms on the counter I call J.P.
—What the hell . . . ?
—I was thinking . . .
—Use this towel.
—Ah. . . .
Jean could have been a nurse. —Here. Try ice.
—What an idiot I am.
—Press hard.
—I did that already.
—Let me see . . . God, woman. . . . You're going to need stitches.

—I wasn't thinking . . . or rather I was thinking. . . . I was . . . . Jean, do you begrudge Stephanie her mother?

—Hey, sit down here. Of course not . . . Have you had a tetanus shot recently?

—Two summers ago, I think. I stepped on a nail at the cottage.

—You should get stitches.

—But Jean, I was thinking. . . .

—Wait a minute. . . . okay . . . What?

—What is this?

—What are you talking about?

—I was thinking about our kids . . . how we were married so we don't have a love child. Does that make them un-love children?

—This is no time . . . You're still bleeding like crazy.

—I'm bleeding because I was thinking about that. It seems so sad.

—Look, press harder.

—A deep sadness, a faultlessness, like original sin.

—Not so original.

—Are they necessary, these love mistakes? The beginning of creativity?

—Press hard.

I pound my head against the wall for the pain of his pressure on my hand. —Jean, everything we love, you and I, is born on God's dark side. It inches into the light slowly, if at all. It isn't easy.

—Never mind. . . . We don't do easy well.

—Can you hear the children?

—They're fine.

—They're so happy. Remarkably happy. People remark, don't they, that our children are so happy?

—Not Margaret.

—No? What did she say?

—I'm not to submit Stephanie to my dark side . . . Heh, press harder there.

—What does she think we'll do? Stephanie's a baby.

—Look. Forget it. Our kids are happy. They take the dark side like a good night's sleep.

—For now. But what if...

—I think we should get you to a clinic or something.

—No. It's okay. But what I was thinking was, what if I wrote about them ... the way I wrote about the famine, and then there was another famine.

—For God's sake, Lois. You didn't stop the rain.

—And you ... the war ...

—I didn't cause the war.

—But it did happen ... and you know how I wished Klaus's porch would rip off from the wall? Well, I walked by that house the other day; I was just thinking how everything had changed, or nothing really had changed, maybe it was just me ... Anyway, I was there and it's gone. The porch is gone. So now when I was thinking ... I was thinking about ... just considering how a drunk driver might meet one of our children out there on the sidewalk....

J.P. is no longer tenderly holding my finger but has grabbed my wrist and slightly twists it. I register that I have made a mistake. —Don't. Stop.... No...

He pushes me against the wall to still my voice, which is not what he intends to do, but to stop the thought. Now I don't fight for it, as I did against the knife. I fall first against the wall, then become a pile of wet clothing on the floor, whimpering. —It was just an idea. I'm sorry.

Jean-Philippe seems sorry too. He sits down on the floor next to me and we are quiet for a moment. My finger drips blood on the front of his shirt.

—Jean, if you ever push me again I'll push you back, and harder.

—Was it one of your children, Lois, or was it mine?

—Yours, of course.

He lifts me off the floor, wipes my face with a wet cloth, and I wipe his. We stand apart from each other and check each other for wounds or a perceptible lack of composure, then go outside to check on the children. By some miracle, there is no traffic whatsoever on the street this afternoon.

*

—Here, could you hold Stephanie a minute? I left her bottle in my room...

I put down my book, still open, on the table. —Sure. Hey, girl, suck on my finger. Hmmm....

—Okay. I'll take her back.

—Watch the burp.

—Gotcha.

—Where are you going?

—The liquor store. You want something?

—No. Oops... Sorry.... She burped down your back. Turn around and I'll wipe it.

—Thanks. I've got some time. How's it going?

—You want some tea? Something to eat?

—Sure. I'm not disturbing you?

—I was going to finish this book before I have to return it. You want me to take Stephanie to the library when I go?

—What is it?

—The book? Ah, just another one of these... Hey, maybe you can tell me. What do you think "biblical beauty" means?

—I don't know.

—This guy here refers to "an almost biblical beauty." What's beautiful in the Bible?

—The poetry? I don't know. A lot of rutting and begetting; that's what comes right off the top.

—I don't think that's what he's referring to.

—What's the context?

—A family starving to death.

—And he calls it biblical beauty? You want me to reheat some of this soup?

—No, but let me hold Stephanie before you drop her in the pot.

A photograph. The image recurs as if it is a photograph I take out of a book and hold in my hand. I am coming home late at night, standing in the hall in the dark. The image is framed by the door to the flat which is ajar because I opened it to come in, but I haven't yet come in. Jean-Philippe is sprawled out on the sofa in half-darkness, asleep. Stephanie has pinned him down; even in his sleep he is careful not to move beneath her or she will wake up. He is pinning her down on his chest, his wide palm resting on her diaper. She doesn't move and fall off his chest. Neither of them awakens when I enter the flat. I don't disrupt the image. I slip in and shut the doors behind me, first the door to the flat, then the door to my room.

*

—Perhaps I should go meet Charlotte. I did a terrible thing leaving her like that. She didn't want to let me go . . .

—But Stephanie was being born.

—Oh sure, I had all the right reasons, which compounds the deceit really, don't you think? I mean, how could she argue?

—She could have come with you.

—No way. I wouldn't have let her even if she asked. That would have made things clear, though. I left her crying that afternoon and I didn't even flinch. I knew she could bear suffering more than I could bear comforting her. I packed and she kept crying.

—Jesus, J.P. It sounds awful.

—It was. I threatened her to get her to stop. I felt like the criminal but she was paying the penalty. Sacrificial substitution.

—Christ, I hate scenes.

—Lois, this wasn't a scene. It was utterly formless.

—Then how did you get away?

—Well, she stopped crying. I knew then it was war. We stared at each other and started removing our clothes; never averting each other's stare. She took off her shirt. I took off mine. I unbuttoned my pants; she slipped hers off over her hips.

—Why are you telling me this?

—I don't know. It was so shocking; I mean, I'm not sure if what we did had anything to do with sex. Anyway, then she told me she didn't want me coming to Paris. But I know she does.

—That isn't obvious ... Would you stop looking at me like that?

—Like what?

—Like I'm ugly.

—I don't think you're ugly.

—But if you did, then I'd be ugly, even if I looked exactly as I do, so I am ugly *in potentia* with you, so I hate you looking at me like that ...

*

Jean-Philippe takes me to an exhibit of Diane Arbus's work that is showing at the Ydessa gallery. It's an easy walk from our house and then we leisurely wander through the gallery. I peer into the faces Arbus photographed. —I like the Jewish giant.

—They're looking at each other, his parents and him. That's different.

—Yeah, it isn't as posed.

—I never noticed that about her work. The portraits ...

—Straight on ugly ...

—No. They don't seem ugly. Everyone agreed to participate.

—It makes it kind of funny.

—They're collaborating with her ...

—Did you see Greer?

—That's beautiful, but not one of them is ugly. Just weird.

—And funny. The nudist with the swan glasses . . .

— . . . in love with the camera.

*

—Mom, Diane hit me.

—I did not.

—You did so.

—Well, you deserve it.

—Do not. Mom, Diane lied.

—Mom, he's being a brat. He's knocking the table when I'm trying to write . . . on purpose.

—Am not.

—Are so, you brat.

—Bitch.

—Mom, Daniel called me a bitch.

—Are you a bitch?

—Mom!

—Mom thinks you're a bitch too, bitch.

—Daniel, use that language again and you'll go to your room.

—I'm glad. I'm glad. I want to go to my room.

—Good. Go.

—Mom, don't send him to his room. It was my fault.

—See? She admits it. She was bugging me first.

—So, idiot? I admit it. So drop it.

—Mom, she called me an idiot.

—Did not.

*

One afternoon in early spring Jean-Philippe comes into the kitchen with a bag of stationery, several pads of paper, pens, computer tapes, etc. and he sets them out on the table to make a display.

—I'm going to get down to some serious work here now. It's been too long.

—How long?

—Months.

—Why's that?

—You know perfectly well. You know, your son calls this thing a grief case. No kidding, that's what he thought they're called. Shit, it's dusty. I can write or get laid. It's a bind. Charlotte kept me up all night and I can only work at night. And now I'm drinking too much. Daniel was imitating me this morning... Really embarrassing, the way he copied my hungover movements... Very careful, moving and trying not to move at the same time. It was very funny.

—Ignore Daniel.

—Well, he's artful as hell. You know, some clowns in native tribes do that, imitate an obnoxious bastard's problems. The clown puts the miscreant in his place.

—Daniel should be put in his place.

—No. My behaviour's abominable. It's no good, your kids seeing me acting like this.

—It's sufficient that you feel guilty. You don't actually have to change.

—Well, I'm going to, if only so I get back to work. Or I'll take a job. I'll be out of here soon.

—Where did these lilies come from?

—I bought them.

—Rubrum, aren't they?

—Yeah.

—For Margaret?

—No. She hates lilies. Says they're too funereal.

—Oh.

—I bought them for us.

—Well, thanks.

—Diane and Daniel like flowers?

—Yes. Daniel particularly... white flowers. And me

too. I like lilies.
　—I thought so.

*

—Fuck, Lois. You quit the book? I talked with Frances today and she told me . . . Fuck, I hate being right.
　—I didn't quit.
　—If that's not quitting... My God. Obscene. That's how she described it.
　—I thought of it as prose poetry.
　—Hah!
　—I wish Frances would discuss my projects with me and yours with you instead of mine with you and yours with me.
　—Then I'd never know what's going on.
　—One of us should get a new editor.
　—Both of us should.
　—But not the same one.
　—Do you still have the manuscript? I'd like to see it.
　—No. I gave it to them and they hated it, but they kept it.
　—How did you get all that stuff on William?
　—Mostly from his ex-wife. She gave me their family scrapbook from those years, and the recipe for those beloved butter tarts. I just pasted everything together.
　—Frances is worried about libel charges ... never mind that she thinks it's appalling.
　—It is appalling, but it's fair. There is as much of my family in there as his. I had Daniel's birthday party shot, and the menu from our cruise in the Bahamas. It's kind of funny, really.
　—William was not amused.
　—So what are they doing with it?
　—They're going to produce it without a text. William is writing a short bio for the introduction.
　—That's what I suggested at the outset.

—Why didn't you just do it?

—I did. The visuals are everything. If seeing is believing, then believing makes us stupid. I wanted people to look at photos of starving people and of William and I having a fine life. To say anything would be satisfying. I wanted people to laugh, to feel sick, whatever, but to give them no satisfaction.

—You know what Sontag says: the whole enterprise of modern high art is to reduce our moral queasiness. You believe that? That's what you're doing.

—I know I haven't felt much moral queasiness in years. And I know starvation doesn't make anyone sick any more, except the people who're starving.

—So why did you lie to me?

—What did I lie about?

—You didn't tell me you'd quit. You defended this project, even after you quit.

—I guess I quit long before our discussion; in fact, before you arrived.

—But you never said so.

—You never asked.

—I did. We talked about your work.

—About my book. I said it's going very well.

—But it's not *the* book.

—A book's a book.

—Christ, woman, why can't you just say what you mean?

—I'm trying.

—Then why didn't you just say, "I'm not finishing that famine book."

—Famine was just one chapter in William's book. I'm still thinking about that, but you didn't ask.

—But we talked about it. Or rather, I talked about it and you, it turns out, were talking about another book. There is another book?

—Yes, but can we talk about something else?

—Evidently that's what we do. You talk about something and I talk about something else.

—Let's choose a third topic, something neutral.
—Well, what is that you are actually writing?
—A story.
—A novel?
—Sort of . . . all my best truths are fiction.
—You want to talk about that?
—No, I don't.
—Well, you could have just said so. You could have just said, "I've dumped William's book and I'm working on something else but I don't want to talk about it."
—Can I get you something to drink?
—No. I want to talk about this.
—Well, I don't.
—Okay, what do you want to talk about?
—Your murder mystery. You could have just said, "I'm writing a murder mystery in which I kill Margaret, but I don't want to talk about it."
—So you talk to Frances as well.
—Yes. Two weeks ago.
—And that's what she said? That I kill Margaret?
—What is it you say you're writing?
—Well, it's a lie what she said, but I don't want to talk about it.
—Don't kill her, J.P. Someday Stephanie's going to learn how to read.
—I'm not killing her, for God's sake. And it's not about Margaret. The woman's French. She's fat, but there's lots of fat women. This I know first hand.
—Fine.
—I've been tom-catting around . . . You want to talk about that? Call it research . . . and I've found so many fat women, practically right outside your front window there.
—J.P., this discussion is over.
—No. You should know what's happening in your neighbourhood. Sometimes I score it and sometimes I buy it. I buy it by the pound, for God's sake, and it's sucking me dry. That's why I was talking to Frances today. I need a grant. And

besides my research, I owe you some money too.

—You don't owe me anything.

—They're huge women; three of them working that west corner of Queen. It's paradise.

—J.P.

—Don't start with your waspy scruples, Lois. You compare your tart recipes with starvation, and then climb on my back? I just want to take a look. It's like mining for precious metal, mounds rolling over global rolling hills; you never know where you'll find it, veins running through the ground; you just have to keep digging.

—The story's been done before. It's Percival.

—You must be joking.

—No. Look it up. Anyway, it's all been done, but that one too.

—This is a murder mystery, a trash novel.

—So why kill her?

—I don't.

—Don't lie.

—No, she kills me.

—Oh well, that's better. And does it make her happy?

—No.

—Then it makes you happy?

*

—What's he like?

—He is so completely different from you or me. Maybe that's the hook, the difference. For us even to make love is difficult . . . almost impossible. It's not his wife; that's something else again, very specific, but it doesn't have anything to do with me . . .

—No? Really?

—No. . . . but sometimes I realize it would take the knowledge of a thousand nights of good love and a thousand disasters for me even to begin with him, and still I'd begin knowing nothing. He has to tell me what to do, speak each action first... so deliberate, to free me from my ignorance of his wants. I sometimes shake to think of the humiliation I feel, and still want it...

*

—Are you hungry?
—Why would I be hungry? Of course I'm not hungry.
—I just asked.
—Why'd you ask?
—God, Lois. You've got to get ahold of yourself.
—Ahold of myself? How the hell do you do that? What an idiotic expression.
—What the hell... who did you run into out there?
—Well, think about it! Do you hold yourself?
—Fuck, Lois. That's a little personal.
—Shit, I need something to drink. We have any juice?... No, of course not. The fridge is stuffed but the one thing I want we don't have.
—I'll find it. Slow down.
—Great. First I run into Klaus; we fight. Then Frances. Now you. And it's only two o'clock. I've got to go shopping with Diane to get her skirt... Just great. So there's still her, the saleswomen... and maybe I'll run over a cop...

*

I'm lying on the couch, the children are asleep and Jean-Philippe comes in, finds my face wet and sits down next to me, putting his hand on my back.
—Is there anything I can do?
—No. I've just got to come to terms, literally, make choices.
—Lois, you look so sad.

—It is sad. It's the exact opposite of what I want to do, but it's what I have to do.
—Sure.
—No. It's different for you. Well, in some ways the same. There's always limitations ... right from the start, what we can't have. So we supplant desire with lust, until compassion gives way, and then love, in the bacchanal, happily. Before the drought.
—Shhh ...
—Sorry. No, she's still sleeping.
—Well, it's not a whole book. What comes next?
—Nothing. Well, the drought.

*

—Okay, Lois. I was thinking about what you've said about our homocentric approach here. I've really been working on it and I purged it entirely from the narrative structure in my book. It's no longer a murder mystery. Well, listen up: there's this man who's married to this woman, but they don't love each other, right? He's living with another woman who's married to a man who doesn't love her any more if they ever did which is doubtful. Half of these people are eating all the time and the other half aren't eating hardly at all, so there's your universality, okay? Okay ... Anyway, she's sleeping with yet another man no one knows except maybe her, if anyone knows him at all, which I doubt but that part's not in my story. Okay? So the first man's going to have the talk with his wife, right? He's gone to her place—see, they haven't really been together for a while—and he's going to ask her for a divorce and ask to take their daughter. Did I tell you that part? That they have a daughter?
—I guessed that.
—Okay. All of this he knows is quite beyond her, to give him a divorce and their daughter, but what the hell, it's worth asking, right? She lets him into her apartment and now they're

going to have the talk.

—Look. I don't want to hear you killing Margaret.

—Hey, no. Listen up. He's sitting on a stuffed chair bouncing their baby on his knee, sitting across the room waiting for her to say something from the far side of the room. See there's some distance between them . . .

—Listen, J.P. . . .

—It's fiction, okay? Just listen. Well, the distance, that part's important because once she finally opens her mouth to answer what happens is that there's an earthquake and the ceiling falls in right on top of her and kills her. Okay? But not on him. He's got a kid, they're dusty but unharmed, so he shakes the dust off his jacket and her diaper and leaves . . . Coffee? . . . Wait, there's more. Now the woman he lives with is going shopping at the same time he's supposed to be having this talk with his wife, and there at the end of the street she sees her husband which is totally a coincidence but she figures since he's there just a half-block away they might as well have their talk too, which means that both these talks will be happening simultaneously, right? Now she's walking towards him and he still hasn't even seen her, and she just wants to get it over with when the earth begins to tremble. She jumps back just in time. The ground beneath his feet yawns, opens up and swallows him. He's gone. She turns around to go back home, but the day's not over yet. Her lover, the one no one knows including her, is waiting for her at the bus stop. But she's too weary to hurry, so recently widowed and all, and then there's grief—even bad love is sad when it's over—but through it all or maybe because of the grief she realizes she and he have to have their talk too, as soon as possible. She's expecting her children home from school. I forgot to mention that, that she has two children.

—But I guessed that . . .

—Yeah . . . and she'll have to tell them they've lost their father and she doesn't have much time and wants to get it over with. He sees her and motions for her to hurry, thinking, I suppose, that the loud noise behind him is the streetcar, but it's not. Behind him is a huge tidal wave rolling down the street, which happens sometimes after earthquakes, and she sees it but he doesn't until it sweeps over him, sweeps him up and away but recedes so that the water just barely laps the toes of her black leather boots. She never even gets her feet wet.

—That is still an act of aggression. You made the world eat my lover.

—I can't help how I feel.

*

It is quite late when J.P. puts Stephanie down to sleep. I've switched off my computer and move into the living room, where I find him sucking on a bottle of Chimay, listening to my Marvin Gaye tape, eating a plate of fresh oysters. I take his bottle, swig a mouthful of the ale, and he stands up to take back the bottle, so it begins as a dance. We dance. I place my mouth over his mouth entirely and breathe, taking his breath away. He slides down my body, pulling my pants over my ass, and runs his tongue along my leg. I stoop down onto the rug, squeeze lemon juice onto an oyster and pour it into my mouth. When he kisses my mouth I slip the oyster onto his tongue. I crawl away. Now he's behind me, pulls my hair back and sucks in my breath so one moan is released from two bodies when we exhale. Stephanie, waking up in the next room, also shrieks.

*

The next morning I pull out the rusty bundle-buggy and set out with the children to do our grocery shopping, as we used to do weekly, together. Upon waking, J.P. apparently discovered this piece of writing on the kitchen table and read it:

The language of love is not the language we speak

and even when we speak about love or even in actions of love when we speak (you and I) the language of love is not the language we speak. The sounds of our original loves were once familiar, common speech although we didn't understand the words. The swishing sounds of our primordial loves were a mother's hand travelling across the body of a new baby who had just passed from lizard to human, hushing and licking sounds that are not in our language now.

"Still, still mein süsses, kleines baby," your mother said and mine, "My sweet, thank God you're not affected by my disease" (for you were born in German and I was born in my mother's anxiety)

but now we can't (or won't) utter the sounds. If spoken now at all, it is in loose translation. Now when we speak of love or in love you speak an English hardened and distanced from your mother tongue because your family moved to Canada when you were young, away from your father land and your mother tongue (but isn't this an inversion? isn't the word considered male and the land female?) and as for me, I murmur sounds like a cat's purr because I am neither land nor tongue but breath that has not yet breathed a word of love, yet the anxiety gave way to relaxation, and much later in your arms I even relinquished my fear but still I did not accomplish speech

and in both cases (yours and mine) something is lost; something is always lost in translation

but you are always far ahead of me. Due to age or circumstance and perhaps to the particularity of your intelligence, you passed into English from German when I hadn't yet accomplished any language and sometimes I fear I never will. You speak flawless English but I do not understand your language. You sound certain, but this I surmise from the tone because I do not understand the content. Even when you shout at me it is clear and your anger is sharp, which is what they say about bright minds, and there I am, speechless, because, as they say, you take my breath away but, as I say, perhaps I can't speak anyway and certainly I can't speak the language of love and certainly I can't speak when there is such an absence (which may not be another language but a different vocabulary; I cannot say because I don't understand what it is you're saying; I don't speak the language) of love

(but there are long silences in your speech as well as in mine and I wonder, is this the language of unlove or is it the empty spaces that occur within every language, the silences that are essential to any language, the space between words and thoughts without which there can be no coherent speech? Space in sound is a main constituent of language without which there would be just noise and this must be true of love, of the language of love.)

What are you saying? you demand.

I just wish that I spoke German, not because I want to compete with your speech in your mother tongue any more than in your mother love, but there must be some completion here and it must tie in with its beginnings. We do so badly in English. It is far removed from your beginnings and mine.

Ihab Hassan, a philosopher who travelled away from Egypt into English, asked, "Who reckons the deep declensions of Desire, inflections of the Logos, or denials of a mother's tongue? Does 'matricide' free men into alien speech?" When I asked you the same question you got very angry and said that this would be easy to determine; establish a sample group, people who do not speak their mother tongue. I, again speechless, wondered, Isn't that everyone? and you took my silence to be stupidity and you said that I was asking a simple empirical question which is odd since I show little interest in answers to empirical questions.

O God, my God, what can I say? Apparently nothing

but I am still curious; if not our mother tongue, what language will take us into speech that can be a language of love when it is not the language we speak? Surely we need a whole body of language; it must be a whole body that can replace a mother tongue. It must have a solid torso connecting head to hands, legs winding sinuously up into its buttocks, a meeting place of penis and vagina bound to a uterus that grows round with this new tongue that breaks into the air and cries when the cold air fills its lungs for the first time.

This is not a mother's tongue, the primordial yelp at the first sign of life and love. It is an infant's body of language we are first given, first speak. O God, o God, we are so ignorant too. How do we begin to speak this language of love when we cannot yet speak? The infant's body curls up around the word as if in some pain.

This is some beginning; the labium stretches until it is all opening to let the head (which seems impossibly large) through. Then immediately it closes in tight behind our crooked legs

and we howl. Speech comes much later. First, we wail.

*

I return with Diane pulling the bundle-buggy full of packages into the kitchen, Daniel behind me weighed down with bags, and we find J.P. sitting at the kitchen table, the pages rolled into a scroll in his hands. He is clearly annoyed. Diane starts:
　　—Hi, J.P. You won't believe all the stuff we bought. Mom wants to make dinner. She wants to make lots of dinners.
　　—Lois, what the hell is this?
　　—Kids . . . Is Stephanie asleep?
　　—Yes.

—Daniel, why don't you go check on her.
—I said she's asleep.
—Kids, you go outside. I'll put this stuff away.
—I've got to practise my clarinet.
—Practise outside.
—Mother, that's dumb. People will stare.
—Practise later.
—I'll go to Margot's.
—Daniel, go outside.
—I don't have anywhere to go.
—Go skateboard.
—The wheel's broken.
—Go fix it.
—I'm hungry.
—Here, take this bagel and go.
They roll their eyes and leave.
—What is this?
—That?
—This. I can't believe it, Lois. What the fuck are you doing?
—We went shopping.
—I mean with this.
—I'm not doing anything.
—You left it here.
—Yeah ... well, I just finished it ...
—Well, why did you show it to me?
—I didn't.
—You left it on the table. I was sure to read it.
—I didn't ask you to read it.
—But this is stuff we've talked about. Everything in this piece is what we talked about.
—Yes. We talk about things I think about. I write about things I think about. That isn't a coincidence.
—But I'm not German.
—Of course not.
—This is what we talked to each other about in English, not German. These issues are between you and me. You wrote

143

some things I said.
—You want me to attribute the quote?
—Fuck, Lois.
—Well, is that your problem? An authorial claim? Okay. Fine. I'll put that in: this is Jean-Philippe's thought as well as mine. Okay?
—No.
—I thought we'd come to an understanding.
—You did, did you? You informed me.
—I chose.
—Chose.
—To take it out there where it belongs. This is a break for me, Jean.
—A break, is it?
—I make my own choices. I'm free to do that.
—Fine. And you choose a German prick.
—I have a German lover, out there, yes.
—I know that.
—So what's the problem?
—You showed this to me, about him. We talked about these things right here. Right at this table.
—Look, Jean.
—Right here. It's between us.
—There's no property rights to a conversation.
—You wrote this to that German guy, about my relationship with you, except it's about your relationship with him, and you show it to me?
—I didn't write it to anyone. It isn't a letter.
—Then what the hell is it?
—I was thinking.
—Then why did you show it to me?
—I didn't.
—You left it on the table. I was sure to read it.
—I didn't ask you to read it.
—You left it on the table. You knew I would. You wanted me to read it.
—Yes.

—Why?

—Because I knew you'd understand.

—I understand. Sure, I understand. We've talked about this. It's between you and me. It's all about us.

—But I'm taking it out there. I can do what I want.

—Are you going to show it to that German bastard?

—No.

—Why not? Why didn't you show it to him instead of to me if it's about him?

—It's not about either of you, really. It's my idea.

—But he's in it. You talk about him. Why not leave it on his kitchen table instead of mine.

—In fact, J.P., I left it on my kitchen table, if it's come to that, appropriation of material.

—Okay, your table.

—Leave that aside. I won't show it to him because he wouldn't understand.

—Of course he wouldn't. He wasn't there. I bet he doesn't even know Hassan. Has he read Hassan?

—No, but then neither have you.

—Did he really say that, about establishing a sample group? I didn't say that.

—No, you wouldn't. He would. See?

—What the hell are you doing with a man like that?

—That's between him and me. It's none of your business.

He shakes the papers at me. —But this... this is between us.

—Yes, I guess that's true.

—Of course it's true!

—I knew you'd understand.

*

Three days later I come home to find that J.P. has moved his and Stephanie's belongings out of the flat. He has left several gifts

145

for Diane and Daniel with a thoughtful note explaining that he needs his own place, and that they can visit Stephanie at his place on weekends and Tuesday afternoons when she is with him. The last piece of correspondence between us is pinned to my pillow, typifying the manner in which form, over time, comes to contradict content:

10 April, 1991

Dear Lois,

    I hate you.

    Love, J.P.

AFTERWORD

When Stephanie was returned to mother, Jean-Philippe took an apartment near theirs to facilitate a shared custody arrangement. Frances informs me that he is hoping Margaret will permit him to take Stephanie to Paris with him when he joins Charlotte for a few weeks this summer. Klaus returned to Germany late in the spring, according to plan. His wife is remaining in Canada. Michael will remain in England indefinitely.

The men's leave-taking made little difference to me, except at first, before I conjured them back to argue and converse as before. If anything, we are more intimate now. See, I do better with them without them. When I think or write, one praises, one presses me, demanding more precision of my opinions:

I can see where that might lead, but can you demonstrate it?

to which I sink or rise.

Even my senses have become more acute. I've grown antennae; vibrations indicate Jean-Philippe's ghostly presence, measure Klaus's heart rate. I feel everything more clearly now, the pattern of the wool against my bare legs, a man's fingertips waking me up in my dream, although I sleep alone. I'm wet, am crying in my sleep "I'm really sorry" sometimes, or "Oh yes, thanks."

The children will join Michael in England for the summer, ostensibly so I that I will be able to complete my book. However, this book is finished already

and even as I write the civil war in Ethiopia is ending. After nearly thirty years, the politicians attempt to end the war around a table in London while the armies conclude it in the streets of Addis Ababa

and there is no afterwards. After words is silence

so what I will do in this summer's heat is tend my garden, waste not, want not, hope for rain and for pleasure.

THE APPENDICES

The appendix (veriform) is a hollow muscular tube continuous with the cecum, the first region of the large intestine. In larger mammals the organ is capable of trapping cellulose to be subjected to prolonged digestion.

The function of the literary appendices is midway between that of the large mammal and the human's, whose small, vestigial organ is anatomically archival, consisting of lymphatic tissue similar to that of the tonsils, and similarly susceptible to bacterial infection or swelling due to its limited blood supply.

I make notes and store up cellulose from newspapers, literary sucrose, not easily digested. Hence, journalism finds its way into my appendix:

APPENDIX I.
Famine Persists in Eritrea: A Journalist's Report, Summer 1990

Famine once again threatens the lives of millions in Eritrea, the northern province of Ethiopia. The conditions that caused the 1984 famine have not significantly changed, the civil war that has lasted nearly 30 years continues, and the United Nations has announced a 100 percent crop failure. By conservative estimates, 700,000 metric tonnes of grain (150,000 more than was required at the peak of the 1984 famine) are necessary in order to avert an unprecedented disaster in Eritrea and Tigray.

As of April 1990 the international community had pledged just 90,399 metric tonnes of food to the Eritrea cross-border channel. Three times that amount could be delivered to some of the worst-stricken areas if food was made available.

The prolonged war has played a significant role in creating famine conditions and impedes relief effort. In fact, some observers claim that, in the last decade, famine has been added to the arsenal of weapons in the civil war.

The conflict has its roots in the arrangement made in the wake of WWII, when a UN Commission recommended Eritrea be federated with Ethiopia, "having its own legislative, executive and judicial powers in the field of domestic affairs" (Res 390, 1950).

Conflict ensued when Eritrean newspapers were censored, trade unions and political parties suppressed, the two official languages of Eritrea, Tigrinya and Arabic, were replaced by Amharic, and some factories in Eritrea were transferred to Ethiopia's capital, Addis Ababa. In 1962 the federation was dissolved, Ethiopia annexing Eritrea, and the Eritrean Liberation Front (now the EPLF) was formed.

Ethiopia's Emperor Haile Selassie was overthrown in 1974, in part a result of the 1973-74 famine. Power was seized by the Derg but martial law remained in force in Eritrea. The civil war entered a new phase when the Soviet Union intervened in 1977 on behalf of Ethiopia against Somali forces in Ogaden, and then deployed their troops in Eritrea, necessitating a strategic withdrawal of the EPLF from the towns they had held.

Recently, the Eritrean Relief Association reports that there has been a renewed wave of air raids over civilian targets in Afabet and Massawa. From April 3rd to the 8th, 1990, at least 82 civilians were killed and another 220 wounded.

While still pursuing its military strategy, the EPLF continues its relief efforts and political program, which includes economic and agricultural development, education and more accessible medical care for the population in EPLF-controlled areas.

Meanwhile, the Ethiopian government, as well as the international community and food aid agencies who failed to respond to early warnings in 1983, are not mobilizing against the potentiality of famine. In 1984 appropriate action was taken only once word and images of mass starvation finally reached a responsive public outside of Ethiopia.

APPENDIX II.
The True Words Of Margaret Desjardins

"It's snowing and when it stops it will be raining. Then it will be hot as hell here all summer. Look, I'm not complaining that we moved to Montreal . . . I know it's worse in Winnipeg . . . I love my country, but no, I don't want to go outside just now."

*

"I don't have to know what people are saying. Mostly what people say is nothing but vocal grease. It means nothing; it means 'excuse me'."

*

"Dear, this isn't writing; it's exhibitionism."

*

"I did learn a bit of Polish as a kid. I wanted to talk to Grandma. Actually, all she ever said she said first with her eyes. What? Oh, she said, 'I love you, baby.'"

*

"You think I misunderstand? I don't think so. Nor do I think the artist feels misunderstood because you fail to clearly explain what it is you are trying to do. Those explanations, clear or garbled, are still gibberish. I think it's simply that you fail to do well whatever it is you're trying to do. So actually, it's you who misunderstand."

*

"No, I don't think God made sex to make you miserable . . . No, I don't think there's any meaning in it at all; it just is."

APPENDIX III.
Selected Bibliography

Samuel Beckett, *Three Dialogues*, J. Caler, London, 1965.
"There are many ways in which the thing I am trying in vain to say may be tried in vain to be said."

Jean Cocteau, *La Mort et Les Statues: Photographies de Pierre Jahan*, Éditions Seghers, Paris, 1977.
"Cet homme politique en redingote, cet alligator se sont rencontrés dans le mauvais rêve d'un poète.
"C'est la fin. ROME CAPITULE.
"Les soldats de Cléopatre retournent dans la boue du Nil."

Mary Ellmann, *Thinking About Women*, Harcourt, Brace & World, Inc., New York, 1968.
"In exhaustion or illness, or shortly after sexual intercourse, each person approaches that point of detachment in which human sexuality appears in its essential simplicity and multiplicity—the two forms and the one union between them, repeated in every time and place of human life. But this is an apparition which the slightest encounter with another person, or even the thought of such an encounter, or only a revivified sense of the person's own body by itself, immediately erases. Detachment is gone, and involvement so thorough that one is ordinarily no more conscious of the monotony of sex than he is conscious, in breathing, of the monotony of air."

Peter Gill, *A Year in the Death of Africa: Politics, Bureaucracy and the Famine*. Paladin, Grafton Books, London, 1986.
"Perhaps the problem is one of language. Left to itself, officialdom the world over has a matchless way with words. 'If you can't quite remember what "starvation" is—bring in an international expert and he will tell you,' G.N. Vogel, former executive director of the UN's World Food Programme once observed. 'It's to do with "Groups of the population which,

because of insufficient income or for other reasons, were previously prevented from translating an inherent need for food into actual consumption.""

Ihab Hassan, *Out of Egypt: Scenes and Arguments of an Autobiography*, Southern Illinois University Press, Carondale, Il., 1986.
"The important questions before the human race are not literary questions. They are questions of consciousness—reason, dream, love."

"Imagination may yet prove to be the teleological organ of evolution."

Frances Moore Lappé and Joseph Collins, *World Hunger: Twelve Myths*, Grove Press, New York, 1986.
"Since hunger results from human choices, not inexorable natural forces, the goal of ending hunger is obtainable."

Janet Malcolm, *Diana & Nikon: Essays on the Aesthetic of Photography*, David R. Godine, Boston, 1980.
" If 'the camera can't lie,' neither is it inclined to tell the truth since it can reflect only the usually ambiguous, and sometimes outright deceitful, surface of reality. The history of the medium is the history of its practitioners' struggle to overcome this disinclination, to provide the missing sense of verisimilitude, to bridge the abyss between the viewer's innocent expectations—aroused by his belief in the authority and authenticity of what a photograph shows—and the camera's stubborn refusal to fulfil them."

Susan Sontag, *On Photography*, Ferrar, Straus and Giroux, New York, 1977.
"Photography implies that we know about the world if we accept it as the camera records it. But this is the opposite of understanding which starts from *not* accepting the world as it looks... In contrast to the amorous relation, which is based on how something looks, understanding is based on how it functions.

And functioning takes place in time, and must be explained in time. Only that which narrates can make us understand."

The Talmud
   "We do not see the world as it is; we see the world as we are."

PRINTED IN CANADA